KINGS COOKING STUDIO COOKBOOK

Patricia Mikell, Executive Director for Kings

Susan Loden, cooking studio Manager

Produced by Sillery & Partners, Inc.—Matthew Steele, Project Manager; Gerald
    Twardy, Production Manager; Louis Del Pizzo, Art Director

GRAPHIC DESIGNER: Richard Oriolo

PHOTOGRAPHY: Charles Gold

FOOD STYLING: Polly Talbott, CCP

PROP STYLING: Sylvia Lachter

RECIPES: Kings cooking studio staff. Additional copy by Polly Talbott, CCP

PRODUCTION: Westchester Book Services

We urge everyone, including the most experienced cooks and chefs, to become aware
of the most up-to-date information concerning food selection, storage, handling, and
safety. One of many good sources for this information is the Centers for Disease
Control of the U.S. Department of Health and Human Services. Information is avail-
able from the CDC address or Web site.

CDC, Centers for Disease Control and Prevention

1600 Clifton Road

Atlanta, GA 30333

404-639-3534

1-800-311-3435

Web site: www.cdc.gov/ncidod/op/food.htm

CONTENTS

In celebration of the lives of Joseph and Beatrice Bildner

—*Mr. Joe and Mrs. "B," founders of Kings Super Markets*

How is a passion for great food measured? At Kings cooking studio, it's by the teaspoon, the cup, the dollop, and the dash. It's in the voices of the remarkable chefs who have come to share their love for great cooking and on the faces of every food lover who joins us to listen and learn.

The Kings cooking studio first began classes in 1983, with the simple notion that loving good food like nobody's business meant sharing that love with shoppers in ways they could touch and taste, right in our stores. We wanted them to take home not only the ingredients for great dishes, but also the real joy of creating truly memorable meals. And so the Kings cooking studio was created, the first of its kind ever seen in an East Coast supermarket.

In addition to classes such as "Cooking with Confidence," the curriculum included courses that reflected the times we lived in—"Microwave Mastery" and "Taming the Food Processor." These days, the remarkable diversity of our country is reflected in the studio's wide variety of cooking themes. "Tastes of the Mediterranean" and "French Bistro Cooking" are just two wonderful examples of how far the studio—and the world's cooking—has come.

In addition to fantastic cooking classes, Kings cooking studio has had the great privilege of hosting dozens of world-class chefs including the great French master Jacques Pepin, Michael Romano of New York's famous Union Square Café, and Chris Schlesinger, television host and co-founder of "John and Earl's," an award-winning American barbecue restaurant. All of these teachers have shared their extraordinary skills and creativity with us in unforgettable ways.

It is with great pride that we bring many of their marvelous recipes—and no small measure of their passion for great cooking—to the pages of this book, a collection of favorites that any cook, novice or notable, will enjoy creating. We hope you'll share these recipes with friends and family for years to come.

A senior student we know once said, "I'll be learning new ways to cook until I can't see the pots any more." From all of us at the Kings cooking studio, thank you for sharing your wonderful passion with us for over twenty years.

And now, aprons on.

SUMMER

JEAN YUEH, a native of Shanghai, is a culinary consultant who teaches and writes about Asian cuisines. One of her cookbooks won a Tastemaker Award in the Oriental category. She has traveled to Thailand and Southeast Asia to study with noted chefs and teachers.

East Meets West

Jean Yueh

Shrimp Ravioli (LEFT)

Spinach and Orange Salad (ABOVE)

Grilled Swordfish with Shabu Sauce (FACING PAGE)

Stir-fried Snow Peas

Rice Pilaf with Bok Choy

Candied Ginger Lemon Cookies

3

40 thin round wonton wrappers

1 cup carrots, peeled and shredded

1 cup fennel, shredded

FILLING MIXTURE

1 pound shrimp with shells

6 dry Chinese mushrooms

12 water chestnuts, minced

4 teaspoons ginger, minced

4 tablespoons coriander, chopped

1½ teaspoons salt or to taste

1 teaspoon sugar

½ teaspoon ground white pepper

1 tablespoon sake

SAUCE MIXTURE

1 cup sake

2 cups clam juice

4 slices ginger

4 cloves garlic

2 stalks lemon grass, cut into 1½-inch sections

⅔ cup coconut milk

⅓ cup heavy cream (or use coconut milk)

1 teaspoon curry powder or to taste

2 teaspoons cornstarch in 4 teaspoons water

1 tablespoon lemon juice or to taste

½ teaspoon salt or to taste

Shrimp Ravioli

Soften the dry mushrooms with boiling water, remove hard stems, and mince the caps. Shell the shrimp, devein, wash, drain, and blot dry with paper towels, then mince coarsely. Combine all the ingredients for filling mixture in a bowl, making sure they are well mixed.

To make the sauce, in a saucepan heat sake, clam juice, ginger, garlic, and lemon grass to boiling. Let them simmer for 10 minutes or until there is only 1½ cups of liquid left. Remove the ginger, garlic, and lemon grass. Add coconut milk, cream, and curry powder. Cook until the sauce is reduced to about 2 cups. Add carrots and fennel, and cook for 30 seconds, then thicken the sauce with the cornstarch and water mixture. Add lemon juice and salt; season to taste. Keep warm and serve with the cooked ravioli.

Place about 1 heaping teaspoon filling on a wonton wrapper. Wet half of the edge with water. Bring the dry edge over and seal tightly to form a half moon ravioli. Place on a tray dusted lightly with flour. Repeat with the rest of the filling. Bring a large pot of water to boiling, and cook the ravioli in several batches.

Cook for about 3 to 4 minutes until the shrimp is cooked. Drain well in a colander; if necessary, remove excess water by placing the ravioli on a dry dish cloth. Then quickly remove ravioli to a serving platter.

Pour the sauce over the ravioli, placing some carrot and fennel shreds on top. Serve as an appetizer or as a main course.

Jean Yueh

Wonton wrappers are a great way to make ravioli without creating your own pasta. This delicious Shrimp Ravioli uses Asian ingredients, but try them with any ravioli filling. Just be sure to moisten the edges and seal them carefully so they don't open while you are cooking them. Sauce them right after cooking and try not to stack them, as they can stick together.

Spinach and Orange Salad

Remove the hard stems from spinach. Wash the spinach, drain, and spin dry the leaves. Break leaves into bite-size portions.

Grate the orange rind with a fine grater. With a knife, remove the orange skin and the white pith, then separate the segments from the internal membranes by slicing down to the core on either side of each segment until the segment comes loose. Cut segments into bite-size pieces.

Mix honey, orange juice, lemon juice, soy sauce, olive oil, orange rind, ginger, and pepper flakes in a bowl until well blended.

Just before serving, place spinach and orange in a large bowl; pour the desired amount of dressing over and toss until leaves are well coated with the dressing. Place salad on a serving platter.

Jean Yueh

½ pound fresh spinach

2 large navel oranges

2 tablespoons honey

2 tablespoons orange juice

2 tablespoons fresh lemon juice or to taste

2 tablespoons soy sauce or to taste

2 tablespoons olive oil

½ teaspoon orange rind, grated

1 tablespoon fresh ginger, finely minced

¼ to ½ teaspoon crushed red pepper flakes or to taste (optional)

Grilled Swordfish with Shabu Sauce

1 pound swordfish steak
(1-inch thick)

1½ cups onion, peeled and
sliced

1½ tablespoons ginger, finely
shredded

¼ cup hot Italian pepper
(optional), sliced

¼ teaspoon salt or to taste

¼ teaspoon ground black
pepper or to taste

¼ cup coriander leaves,
chopped (or use Italian
parsley)

2 tablespoons cooking oil

SHABU SAUCE

1 tablespoon wasabi paste or
to taste (use 2 tablespoons
wasabi powder mix with 2½
tablespoons water to make a
paste. Make more if you like to
serve extra wasabi on the side.)

3 tablespoons soy sauce or to
taste

2 tablespoons mirin (Japanese
sweet rice wine) or ½
teaspoon sugar plus water

1 tablespoon lemon juice or to
taste

1 teaspoon rice vinegar

4 tablespoons heavy cream
(or water)

Make wasabi paste for Shabu Sauce. Let it stand for at least 10 minutes or longer, then make Shabu Sauce by combining all the ingredients. Can be done ahead.

Preheat a grill or broiler until very hot. Season swordfish with salt and ground pepper. Cook about 4 minutes on each side, depending on the thickness of the fish and the intensity of the heat. In the meantime, heat the oil in a skillet until hot. Add ginger, onion, and hot pepper. Sauté over medium heat until onion is golden or caramelized. Keep warm until the fish is done; spoon the onion mixture on top of the fish and serve with Shabu Sauce. If desired, serve with additional wasabi paste on the side.

Jean Yueh

Stir-fried Snow Peas

Wash and string the snow peas. Discard the strings.

Toast the sesame seeds in a small skillet over medium heat until golden, being careful not to burn.

Melt the butter over medium heat, then add snow peas, salt, and sugar. Cook until snow peas are heated through and still crisp. Adjust seasoning to taste. Add sesame seeds and toss until well mixed.

Jean Yueh

½ pound fresh snow peas

4 teaspoons sesame seeds, toasted

1 tablespoon butter (or cooking oil)

¼ teaspoon salt or to taste

1 tablespoon sugar

Rice Pilaf with Bok Choy

Toast the almonds in a preheated 325°F. oven for 5 to 8 minutes or until slightly golden, but not burned. Can be done ahead.

Heat oil in a 4 quart or larger pot over medium heat. Add rice and toss until all the rice grains are coated with oil. Add garlic and toss to mix, being careful not to burn the garlic and the rice.

Add chicken broth and turn heat to high until the liquid is boiling. Add carrots, bok choy, lemon grass, turmeric, sage, and salt. Bring back to a boil. Cover the pot and cook the rice over very low heat for 25 to 30 minutes. Remove from the heat, and let it rest for 10 minutes. Add chopped coriander or parsley, and toss to mix. Sprinkle toasted almonds on top and serve.

Jean Yueh

1 cup almond slivers

3 cups long grain rice

2 tablespoons cooking oil

1 tablespoon garlic, minced

4 cups chicken broth

1 cup carrots, diced

1 pound bok choy, chopped

1½ teaspoons turmeric

1 teaspoon ground sage

¾ teaspoon salt or to taste

½ cup coriander leaves, coarsely chopped (or substitute with Italian parsley)

Candied Ginger Lemon Cookies

1 cup plus 2 tablespoons all-purpose flour, sifted

1½ teaspoons baking powder

⅛ teaspoon salt

1 tablespoon lemon peel, grated

½ cup butter (1 stick)

¾ cup plus 3 tablespoons sugar

1 large egg

1 teaspoon vanilla extract

6 tablespoons candied ginger, minced (or to taste)

2 baking sheets

Parchment paper

If a food processor is used, sift flour by processing with steel blade for 30 seconds. Remove from the bowl. Measure 1 cup plus 2 tablespoons of this sifted flour. Return to the bowl and process with baking powder and salt until mixed, about 10 seconds. Remove from the bowl. (Otherwise sift flour, baking powder, and salt together). Grate the lemon peel (or, with a potato peeler, carefully peel the lemon skin without including the white part underneath. Cut them into fine strips, then mince finely.) Mince candied ginger; it is easier to cut them with scissors. Toss with 1 tablespoon of sugar to separate the ginger pieces.

Cream butter and ¾ cup sugar with a mixer. Add egg, vanilla, and lemon peel and beat until well mixed. Add the flour mixture, then beat or process until blended. Add and mix the candied ginger into the batter. Refrigerate the dough for about 2 hours or until firm enough to handle.

Preheat oven to 350°F.

Line 2 baking sheets with parchment paper. Cut the dough into 36 pieces. Roll each piece into a ball (dust hands with flour if the dough gets sticky). Place on the parchment paper, leaving the balls about 1½ inches apart. Place 2 tablespoons sugar in a bowl. Moisten the bottom of a soup spoon in water, then dip the bottom into the sugar. Press the bottom of the spoon onto 1 dough ball, flattening to ⅓-inch thickness. Repeat flattening with remaining dough, dipping spoon into sugar before flattening each ball.

Bake cookies until golden brown, about 18 minutes. When cool, remove cookies from the paper.

Jean Yueh

KATHLEEN K. SANDERSON, a graduate of the California Culinary Institute, is Consulting Food Editor of *Restaurant Business* magazine. In addition, Kathleen serves as a consultant to several food companies.

The Summer Buffet

Kathleen K. Sanderson

Antipasto Skewers

Gorgonzola and Walnut Spread

Lemon Rosemary Chicken with Tomato Vinaigrette

Roasted Vegetable and Pasta Salad (ABOVE)

Hazelnut Orange Biscotti (LEFT)

Antipasto Skewers

1 package golf ball-size
mozzarella balls

2 cloves garlic, chopped

3 tablespoons olive oil

2 tablespoons chopped parsley

Salt and pepper to taste

One 7-ounce jar of roasted red
peppers, drained or 2 red
peppers, roasted

26 basil leaves

13 slices prosciutto

26 toothpicks

This recipe is designed for
the perfect no-stress party.
Make everything ahead of
time and serve at room
temperature. No ovens, no
refrigerators. Just relax and
enjoy your guests.

Drain mozzarella balls and set aside. Combine garlic and olive oil. Stir in parsley, salt, and pepper. Pour dressing over mozzarella balls and toss to coat. Let stand at least 20 minutes.

Cut peppers into 1-inch cubes. Cut prosciutto slices in half. Place 1 mozzarella ball (reserve excess dressing) on each toothpick, followed by red pepper cube, basil leaf, and folded prosciutto. Drizzle skewer with excess dressing and serve.

Kathleen K. Sanderson

Bruschetta

Combine oil with garlic and brush onto one side of the bread. Bake for 8 to 10 minutes or until bread is golden. Keep bruschetta in an airtight container for 1 to 2 weeks.

1 loaf Italian or French bread

⅓ cup olive oil

3 cloves garlic, minced

Gorgonzola and Walnut Spread

Makes 1½ Cups

Combine all of the ingredients for the spread and mix well.

Spread 1 tablespoon of mixture on bruschetta and serve hot or cold. Bake topped brushetta in a pre-heated 400°F. oven for 6 to 8 minutes.

Preheat oven to 400°F. Slice bread in ½-inch rounds on the bias (18 to 20 slices). Place bread slices on a sheet pan.

Kathleen K. Sanderson

6 ounces Marscapone cheese

4 ounces Gorgonzola, crumbled

½ cup toasted walnuts, chopped

¼ cup sun-dried tomatoes (oil soaked), minced

¼ cup chives, chopped

Fresh cracked pepper to taste

Lemon Rosemary Chicken with Tomato Vinaigrette

Serves 8 to 10

In a bowl combine lemon juice, garlic, parsley, rosemary, lemon zest, and red pepper flakes, mix well. Whisk in oil to create a marinade. Season and reserve until ready to use.

Pour marinade over all of the chicken and toss to coat. Let chicken marinate 45 to 60 minutes. Drain chicken, reserving marinade.

Grill or broil chicken 3 to 4 minutes per side, basting with marinade. Cool chicken and garnish with rosemary, lemon slices, and tomato vinaigrette (recipe follows).

Kathleen K. Sanderson

5 whole boneless chicken breasts, split and tenderloins separated

⅓ cup fresh lemon juice

3 cloves garlic, minced

½ cup parsley, minced

3 tablespoons rosemary, minced

1 tablespoon lemon zest, minced

½ teaspoon red pepper flakes

⅔ cup olive oil

Salt to taste

Several rosemary sprigs

1 lemon, sliced

Tomato Vinaigrette

Makes 2½ Cups

⅓ cup red or white wine
vinegar

1 tablespoon Dijon mustard

3 tablespoons shallots
(1 shallot), chopped

1 clove garlic, minced

⅓ cup olive oil

⅔ cup salad oil

2 tomatoes, peeled, seeded,
and chopped (1½ cups)

2 tablespoons parsley, chopped

Salt and pepper to taste

In a bowl combine vinegar, mustard, shallots, and garlic; mix well. Slowly whisk in combined oils. Add tomatoes and parsley. Adjust seasoning and serve with greens, over grilled meats, or tossed with pasta.

Kathleen K. Sanderson

Roasted Vegetable and Pasta Salad

Serves 8 to 10

1 cup olive oil, divided

2 zucchini, large dice (3 cups)

2 yellow squash, large dice
(3 cups)

3 small eggplants, large dice
(2½ to 3 cups)

1 Spanish onion, large dice
(2 cups)

2 red bell peppers

3 to 4 cloves garlic, minced

½ cup parsley, chopped

½ cup basil, shredded

½ cup balsamic vinegar

1 pound penne or rotelle pasta,
cooked al dente

Salt and pepper to taste

Preheat oven to 425°F.

In a large bowl combine ½ cup olive oil with the zucchini, yellow squash, eggplant, onion, and garlic. Toss well to coat. Transfer to a shallow roasting pan and roast for 25 to 30 minutes, turning occasionally.

Broil peppers until charred. Transfer to a paper bag to steam for 4 to 5 minutes. Remove skin from peppers and dice into large pieces.

In a bowl combine herbs, vinegar, and remaining oil. Mix well. Add roasted vegetables, peppers, and pasta. Toss well to coat. Adjust seasoning and serve pasta at room temperature.

Note: If pasta is made in advance, simply toss with a touch of fresh oil and vinegar just before serving to moisten.

Kathleen K. Sanderson

Roasting gives an incredible boost to the already wonderful flavor of fresh vegetables. Choose your favorite vegetables from the market, but always try to be flexible, selecting only the freshest.

Hazelnut Orange Biscotti

2 cups all-purpose flour

½ teaspoon baking soda

½ teaspoon baking powder

¼ teaspoon salt

½ cup softened butter

1 cup sugar

2 eggs

1 teaspoon vanilla

1 tablespoon orange zest

2 cups hazelnuts, toasted and chopped

Flour as needed

The double baking of biscotti makes it seem complicated, but try it once and you'll see that it's not! To skin the hazelnuts, place them on a baking sheet and bake at 350°F. for 15 minutes or until the skin begins to flake off. Then rub the hazelnuts, a few at a time, in a terrycloth dishtowel. Don't worry about the skin that doesn't come off.

Preheat oven to 350°F.

Sift together flour, baking soda, baking powder, and salt; set aside.

In a mixer, cream butter and sugar. Mix in eggs and vanilla. Add orange zest, flour, and nuts; mix to create a dough.

Turn dough onto a lightly floured surface and divide in two equal portions. With lightly floured hands roll dough to create a 12-inch log and place on a lightly buttered cookie sheet. Repeat with remaining dough.

Bake biscotti for 25 minutes (or until golden). Remove from oven and let cool 10 minutes. Cut log on the diagonal into 1-inch cookies (12 per log). Place biscotti, cut side down on cookie sheet, and bake 7 to 8 minutes, turn biscotti and bake another 7 to 8 minutes.

Cool biscotti and place in a cookie tin. Biscotti can be stored for 2 to 3 weeks or frozen for 2 to 3 months.

Kathleen K. Sanderson
Adapted from a Gourmet recipe

ARZU YILMAZ holds a master certificate in catering from New School University. She is experienced in Turkish, French, and Mediterranean cooking and baking. Her recipes and articles have appeared in leading Turkish magazines. A member of NYACP and IACP, Arzu is owner of a catering business, Dainty Palate.

Mediterranean Buffet

Arzu Yilmaz

Baby Eggplants Stuffed with Garlic Tomatoes (ABOVE)

Stuffed Grape Leaves (LEFT)

Circassian Chicken in Paprika Walnut Sauce

Frozen Lemon Parfait Cakes

Ricotta Lemon Rounds with Almond Cream

Baby Eggplants Stuffed with Garlic Tomatoes

6 small Italian eggplants

1 can (16 ounces) diced tomatoes

1 medium onion, thinly sliced

4 cloves garlic, minced

½ bunch parsley (¼ bunch parsley leaves, chopped; ¼ bunch parsley left whole for garnish)

1 tablespoon red wine vinegar

3 tablespoons sugar

1 tablespoon salt

¼ plus ¼ cups olive oil

You'll find baby eggplants in all sizes and they are perfect for stuffing. Adjust the recipe according to how large the eggplants are, giving each person either one large half or two smaller halves.

Fill a large bowl with water. Add 2 tablespoons of salt and stir until salt is dissolved. Peel eggplants making zebra stripes then place them into salted water for 20 minutes. In a medium-size sauté pan, put onions and oil and sauté for a few minutes. Then add tomatoes, vinegar, salt, and sugar; cook for 10 minutes (stir frequently). Add the garlic and chopped parsley. Cook for a few minutes then remove from stove and set aside.

Turn the broiler to high. Drain eggplants and dry them with a paper towel. Arrange them on a grill pan and brush with ¼ cup olive oil. Grill them in the oven until they are golden brown.

Preheat oven to 350°F. Rearrange eggplants in an ovenproof dish, cut the eggplants in half, stuff them with tomato mixture, decorate with parsley sprigs, cover with foil. Bake in the oven for 30 minutes. Let stand for 15 minutes.

You can serve them at room temperature or serve cold. (Cover and keep refrigerated for several days.)

Arzu Yilmaz

Stuffed Grape Leaves

Serves 8

6 cups plus 2 cups water

16 ounces grape leaves

2 large onions, finely chopped

1 cup rice, soaked in warm, salted water for 20 minutes

3 tablespoons currants, soaked in water

2 tablespoons pignolia nuts

½ cup fresh mint leaves, chopped

½ cup olive oil

1 tablespoon allspice

1 tablespoon cinnamon

2 tablespoons sugar

2 lemons, cut into wedges

Place 6 cups of water in a sauce pan and bring to a boil. Unroll grape leaves and place them in the boiling water. Boil for 5 minutes. Take them out to drain in a colander. Separate leaves one by one without breaking. Remove stems and place leaves around the rim of the colander.

To make the filling, in a large pan, sauté onions and pignolia nuts in olive oil until golden (15 to 20 minutes). Drain and rinse rice. Add in the onions. Sauté for 5 more minutes. Add currants, spices, and mint. Add 1 cup of water, cover with lid, and bring it to a boil. Reduce heat and simmer for 10 to 15 minutes. Let it cool.

Place a few grape leaves on the bottom of a wide pan. Lay the rest of the leaves on a flat surface and place a spoonful of the rice mixture in the middle of each. Fold the near end of each leaf over the mixture, then the side flaps to seal it in. Roll it up into a thin cigar.

Arrange the stuffed grape leaves in the pan, pack tightly, and pour the remaining cup of water over them. Cover with a lid.

Bring the liquid to a boil. Reduce heat. Cook gently for one hour. Leave it to cool in the pan and serve cold with wedges of lemon.

Arzu Yilmaz

Circassian Chicken in Paprika Walnut Sauce

Serves 8

Combine the poaching ingredients. In a large pot, put chicken pieces into poaching liquid. Bring it to boil then cover and lower the flame; simmer until tender.

Remove chicken from the pan, reservng poaching liquid, let it cool. Strain the poaching liquid and save 2 cups. Cut chicken meat into thin pieces.

To make the walnut sauce, grind the walnuts, spices, and salt in a food processor. Pulse them until they are well mixed. Gradually add the poaching liquid to make a thick pouring consistency. Mix chicken parts with one half of the sauce. Place on a serving platter. Spread the rest of the paste over the chicken. Refrigerate for a few hours. (Sauce will thicken while in the refrigerator.)

To make the paprika oil, warm the oil in a small saucepan over a low heat, then stir in paprika until it turns red. Before serving drizzle this sauce over the chicken and garnish with walnut pieces. This works best when you make it a day before and serve the next day. (Cold or room temperature.) It can be kept for a few days in the refrigerator.

Arzu Yilmaz

One 3-to-3½-pound chicken (cut into serving pieces)

POACHING LIQUID

1 large onion, quartered

1 medium carrot, cut in half

1 stalk celery, cut in half

3 sprigs parsley

2 quarts water

1 teaspoon salt

WALNUT SAUCE

16 ounces shelled walnuts

3 thin slices of white bread, crusts removed, crumbled

1½ tablespoons paprika

¼ teaspoon cayenne pepper

Pinch of salt

2 cups of reserved poaching liquid

PAPRIKA OIL

3 tablespoons walnut oil

2 teaspoons paprika

Walnut halves for garnish

Frozen Lemon Parfait Cakes

Serves 8

8 to 10 lemons

2 cups sugar

8 large egg yolks, plus 2 whole eggs

1 cup unsalted butter, cut into pieces

1½ cups plus 2 tablespoons heavy cream, chilled

Candied lemon zest (recipe follows)

8 ounces crème fraîche

Prepare ice water bath in a large bowl. Juice enough lemons to yield one cup. Juice one additional lemon and reserve juice.

Make lemon curd by placing 1 cup lemon juice, sugar, egg yolks, whole eggs, and butter in a saucepan. Whisk to combine. Cook over medium heat, whisking constantly until mixture begins to boil, about 10 minutes. Strain curd through fine mesh strainer into a bowl. Set in ice bath. Stir periodically until cool; remove from ice bath. Refrigerate at least 1 hour and up to 3 days.

Place 1½ cups chilled heavy cream in a mixing bowl; whisk until soft peaks form. Reserve ½ cup lemon curd for sauce; add remaining curd to whipped cream. Fold gently, combine well.

Place 8 ring molds, 3 inches in diameter and 2¼ inches high, on baking sheet lined with parchment paper. Divide parfait among molds, filling each with ¾ cup. Place in freezer on sheet until firm, at least 4 hours.

LEMON ZEST

4 lemons

2 cups sugar

1 cup cool water

To prepare the lemon zest, remove skin (yellow part only) from lemons with a vegetable peeler, keeping pieces long. Cut into fine julienne. Place them in a small bowl; cover with boiling water. Let stand 30 minutes, drain.

Bring sugar and the cool water to a boil in a small saucepan over medium heat. When sugar is completely dissolved, add julienned zest, reduce heat to low, and cook 10 minutes. Remove from heat and let stand overnight. You can keep this in an airtight container in the refrigerator for up to 2 weeks.

Drain candied lemon zest and reserve syrup. Whisk ½ cup syrup, the reserved ½ cup lemon curd, and juice of one lemon in a small bowl.

Place frozen parfaits on plates. Allow to rest at room temperature 4 to 5 minutes before removing molds. Meanwhile, whisk crème fraîche and remaining 2 tablespoons cream in a bowl until soft peaks form. Remove molds, top with crème fraîche mixture. Garnish with candied zest. Serve.

Arzu Yilmaz

Ricotta Lemon Rounds with Almond Cream

Makes 12 Dozen

Preheat oven to 350°F. Line two baking trays with parchment.

To make the dough, mix butter and sugar in a mixing bowl. Add the eggs one at a time, then add ricotta cheese, flour, baking powder, and vanilla. (It is going to be a soft dough.) Spoon dough rounds onto the baking trays, leaving space between each. Bake in the oven for 30 minutes, until slightly golden.

To make the syrup, combine all the ingredients in a saucepan and bring to a boil. Lower the heat and simmer for 10 minutes, then set aside.

Pour warm syrup over cookies as soon as they are baked. Give them a few turns to absorb the syrup. Refrigerate until cool. Serve with whipped cream and slivered almonds.

Arzu Yilmaz

2 pounds ricotta cheese

3 eggs

⅓ cup sugar

⅓ cup flour (all purpose)

½ cup butter, softened

1 teaspoon baking powder

1 teaspoon vanilla

1 cup whipped cream

1 cup toasted almonds, slivered

SYRUP

2 cups sugar

1½ cups water

1 tablespoon lemon juice

SONDRA SEN has been teaching Indian cuisine at the cooking studio since its inception. She also conducts cross-cultural training for executives planning overseas business trips and is currently working on a cookbook.

Tandoori-Style Grill

Sondra Sen

Tandoori Chicken (ABOVE)

Saffron Rice with Raisins and Almonds (LEFT)

Malai Kopta Curry

Cucumber and Tomato Raita

Coriander Chutney

Tandoori Chicken
Grilled Chicken Marinated in Yogurt and Seasonings

Serves 4

Place chicken pieces in a shallow baking dish. Pierce with a knife in 2 to 3 places on both sides of the chicken.

In a bowl, place garlic, ginger, cumin, coriander, red pepper, and salt, and blend with a spoon. Add yogurt, vinegar, and lemon juice (optional) and blend well.

Rub marinade into gashes in the chicken pieces. Cover and refrigerate overnight or at least 6 hours.

Remove chicken from refrigerator and let stand at room temperature until dish can safely be placed in the oven. Baste the chicken pieces with half the melted butter and bake at 350°F. for 40 minutes.

Remove from the oven, baste with remaining butter, sprinkle with paprika. Broil or grill for 6 to 8 minutes, turning pieces once.

Garnish with roasted cumin seeds and place on a serving dish. Serve with onion rings and lemon wedges arranged over the top or a tomato, onion, and green chili garnish.

Since you might not be able to install a tandoori oven in your home, try this version. Rubbing the marinade into gashes in the chicken and marinating overnight help to create the tandoori flavor of this most favorite of India's chicken preparations.

3½ pounds chicken pieces (breasts, legs, thighs), skinned

MARINADE

2 garlic cloves, minced

1 teaspoon ginger powder

1 teaspoon cumin powder

2 teaspoons coriander powder

½ teaspoon red pepper

1 teaspoon salt

5 tablespoons plain yogurt

1 tablespoon red wine vinegar

2 tablespoons lemon juice (optional)

4 ounces melted butter

½ teaspoon paprika

2 tablespoons cumin seeds

1 onion

Sliced thin lemon wedges

Tomato, Onion, and Green Chili Garnish

Serves 4

Arrange slices of onion rings, tomatoes, green pepper, and lemon wedges on a plate. Place tandoori chicken on top of the arranged vegetables.

Sondra Sen

1 onion, sliced thin

4 small chili peppers, preferably or 1 large chili pepper sliced in strips

2 tomatoes, cut in ½-inch slices

2 lemons, cut in wedges

Saffron Rice with Raisins and Almonds

Serves 4

1 cup long-grain basmati rice

1¾ cups water

½ teaspoon saffron threads

2 tablespoons butter

1 teaspoon salt

3 to 4 whole cloves

¼ stick cinnamon, crushed

½ cup golden raisins

½ cup sliced almonds

Place the ingredients in a heavy one-quart pot. Bring to a boil, reduce heat, cover tightly, and simmer for approximately 20 minutes until rice is tender, but not overcooked. Fluff the rice and serve hot.

Hint: Stir-fry rice in butter for 1 to 2 minutes, then add remaining ingredients.

Sondra Sen

Malai Kopta Curry

t the butter in a heavy saucepan and add onions. Sauté 6 to 8 minutes
lightly browned. Add garlic and sauté 30 seconds.

pepper, coriander, and ½ of ginger and salt. Cook 5 minutes.

atoes and cook until soft, about 5 to 6 minutes.

of the ginger, and sour cream; stir. Add water

ooth.

ream. Simmer
Re

Heat
tas are nd

¾ stick butter

2 cups onion, diced

2 teaspoons garlic, chopped

½ teaspoon red pepper

3 tablespoons ground coriander

3 tablespoons fresh ginger, grated

2 large tomatoes, chopped

1½ tablespoons garam masala

1 pint sour cream (fat free)

2 cups water

2 tablespoons fresh coriander leaves and paprika for garnishing

Salt to taste (about easpoons)

e on 5 to 10 seconds until
, lemon, sugar (optional), and
utney is finely chopped.

Sondra Sen

m

Cucumber and Tomato Raita

Serves 4

1 medium-size cucumber, peeled, seeded, chopped fine, drained

1 medium-size tomato, chopped fine

1 teaspoon salt

2 cups plain yogurt

½ teaspoon cumin powder

½ teaspoon coriander powder

½ teaspoon paprika

Place cucumber and tomato into a bowl. Add salt and toss together gently.

Blend yogurt into the vegetables.

Combine cumin, coriander, and paprika. Sprinkle over the yogurt salad. Refrigerate.

Place in a serving bowl and serve chilled as a side dish.

Sondra S

Coriander Chutney

Makes 1 Cup

3 cups coriander leaves, washed, coarsely chopped, tightly packed

1 garlic clove, peeled

One 2-inch piece of ginger root, scraped

¼ small onion

3 tablespoons lemon juice

1 teaspoon sugar (optional)

½ teaspoon salt (optional)

Put garlic and ginger in a blender. Switch machi
finely chopped. Add onions, coriander leave
salt (optional). Pulse several times until ch

DIANA ALBANESE comes from a family that has owned a food market in Bayonne, NJ, for 75 years. She has been a private caterer and was director of La Cucina D'ana. Diana has studied at the French Culinary Institute and La Technique, and is on the faculty of Brookdale Community College's Creative Cooking Classes.

Meals in Twenty Minutes

Diana Albanese

Vietnamese Summer Rolls with Grilled Shrimp and Vegetables

Chicken Breasts with Garlic and Balsamic Vinegar over Panzanella Salad (LEFT)

Zucchini Fritters

Grilled Caesar Salad (ABOVE)

Zuccotto

Vietnamese Summer Rolls with Grilled Shrimp and Vegetables

Serves 8

¼ pound rice vermicelli

1 tablespoon peanut or canola oil

12 medium shrimp, peeled

1 cup julienned or shredded carrots

3 scallions, white and a bit of the greens, julienned

1 Kirby cucumber, peeled and julienned

1 ripe avocado, peeled and sliced thin

12 cilantro sprigs

24 mint leaves

8 to 10 sheets rice paper (8 inches each) for summer rolls

Soak rice vermicelli in hot water for 10 to 20 minutes or until soft. Drain in a colander.

While noodles are soaking, heat a grill pan on high heat. Add oil and grill shrimp for a minute on each side. When cooled, slice lengthwise.

Place ingredients for the filling in separate piles or bowls.

Soak rice paper for 20 seconds or until softened. Lay on a clean cloth towel.

Fill rice paper with shrimp, carrots, scallion, cucumber, avocado, and top with herbs. Make sure not to overfill. Roll up the paper and cut with a sharp knife into desired lengths. Serve with dipping sauce.

Dipping Sauce

Makes approximately 1 cup

1 tablespoon toasted sesame seeds

½ cup soy sauce

2 tablespoons roasted sesame oil

1 tablespoon rice wine vinegar

1 teaspoon garlic, minced

2 tablespoons fresh ginger, minced

1 teaspoon sugar

Combine all the ingredients in a bowl and stir to blend.

Diana Albanese

Chicken Breasts with Garlic and Balsamic Vinegar over Panzanella Salad

Serves 6

Pound the chicken breasts with a mallet to an even thickness. Set a large fry pan over medium to high heat and add the oil.

Salt and pepper the chicken and dust with Wondra. When the pan is hot, add the chicken and cook until lightly colored, about 3 minutes. Add the garlic and continue cooking until the garlic is just starting to color, about 2 minutes.

Add the vinegar and chicken broth and turn the chicken over. Cover and cook for 5 more minutes. When the chicken is done, remove from the pan and set aside in a plate. Reduce the vinegar mixture until it thickens. Reserve 2 tablespoons for the salad dressing.

Slice the chicken breasts and serve on top of the salad.

CHICKEN BREASTS

6 boneless, skinless chicken breast halves

2 tablespoons canola oil

Wondra flour for dredging chicken breasts

Salt and freshly ground black pepper

6 cloves garlic, peeled

¼ cup balsamic vinegar

¼ cup fresh or canned chicken broth

Panzanella Salad

In a bowl large enough to accommodate the salad, add the balsamic reduction and whisk in the olive oil, salt, and pepper. Combine the bread, tomatoes, onions, cucumbers, and basil leaves in the bowl. Toss together when ready to serve.

Diana Albanese

Panzanella salad, with or without chicken, needs to be made with red-ripe tomatoes and a high quality extra-virgin olive oil. Give the bread a little time to soak up the dressing before serving.

2 tablespoons reserved balsamic reduction

1 cup olive oil

Salt and freshly ground black pepper to taste

6 to 8 slices Tuscan bread, cubed

3 tomatoes cut into small chunks

1 small red onion, sliced thin

1 cucumber, seeds removed, sliced

½ cup basil leaves, preferably the smallest

Zucchini Fritters
Fritelle di Zucchini

Serves 4 to 6

1 pound small zucchini, washed

¼ cup parsley, chopped

1 teaspoon garlic, minced

½ cup freshly grated Parmesan cheese

3 eggs, lightly beaten

1¼ cup fine unflavored breadcrumbs

Freshly ground black pepper

Vegetable oil

Salt

Trim both ends of the zucchini. Using a box grater, shred the zucchini lengthwise using the large holes. Combine the zucchini in a bowl with the parsley, garlic, and grated cheese. Mix the beaten eggs with the zucchini mixture.

Add ¼ cup of the breadcrumbs and the black pepper. If the mixture seems too loose to hold its shape, add some more breadcrumbs and cheese. Spread the remaining 1 cup of breadcrumbs on a plate for dredging.

In a 10-inch skillet or sauté pan, add enough vegetable oil to come to at least ½ inch on the sides. Turn the heat to medium high.

Add salt to taste to the mixture. Shape the zucchini mixture into 3-inch flat patties about ½ inch thick. Dredge them in the breadcrumbs on both sides.

Carefully slip them into the hot oil. Fry until edges are brown and bottoms are golden. Turn over and cook the other side until golden brown.

Using a slotted spatula transfer to paper towels to drain. Make sure not to overcrowd the pan. You will have to cook them in two batches.

Serve hot or at room temperature. This dish can be served with a fresh tomato basil sauce on the side.

NOTE: You can substitute 1 pound of blanched asparagus for the zucchini.

Diana Albanese

Grilled Caesar Salad

In a food processor, add the garlic, anchovies, cheese, vinegar, Worcestershire sauce, mustard, lemon, and pepper. Process until blended.

Scrape down the sides of the processor. With the motor running, slowly add the oil and water. If the mixture is too thick, add a little more water. The dressing can be made ahead and stored in the refrigerator for 1 week.

Preheat the grill or broiler.

Trim the ends of the romaine hearts, but leave intact. Slice the hearts in half lengthwise and place cut side up on a sheetpan or grill. Brush the dressing over the lettuce leaves, making sure that it goes in between the leaves. Sprinkle the pine nuts on the tops of the hearts.

Set the sheetpan on the top shelf in the oven and cook for several minutes or place romaine on grill pan, turning occasionally. The lettuce will start to wilt and brown lightly. Remove promptly from the oven or grill and sprinkle the Parmesan shavings on top. Serve warm.

Diana Albanese

1 large garlic clove cut in half

6 to 8 oil-packed anchovies

3 tablespoons grated Parmesan cheese

1 teaspoon red wine vinegar

1 teaspoon Worcestershire sauce

1 teaspoon mustard

1 teaspoon fresh lemon juice

1 teaspoon freshly ground black pepper

½ cup olive oil

¼ cup water, or more if needed

3 hearts of romaine lettuce

½ cup pine nuts

½ cup shaved Parmesan cheese

Zuccotto

4 ounces shelled hazelnuts

1 family size frozen pound cake, thawed

½ cup dark rum

7 ounces semisweet chocolate chips, medium chopped

2 cups cold heavy cream

¾ cup confectioners' sugar plus more for dusting

Cocoa powder for dusting

Preheat oven to 400°F.

Bake hazelnuts on a sheetpan for 5 minutes until lightly brown. Set aside to cool and chop finely.

Line a round-bottomed 1½-quart stainless steel bowl with a water-dampened piece of cheesecloth, extending over the sides of the bowl.

Cut pound cake into less than ½ inch thick slices. Cut each slice in half on a diagonal, forming two triangles. Place rum in a small bowl and brush cake with the rum. Place the triangles in the bottom and the sides of the bowl lined with cheesecloth. Working all around the bowl, cover any gaps with small pieces of cake.

Divide chocolate in half and melt half in the microwave. Cool slightly. Whip the heavy cream with confectioners' sugar until stiff. Combine with nuts and remaining chopped chocolate.

Fill the bottom and sides of the cake with half the whipped cream mixture, creating a well in the center. Fold the cooled melted chocolate into the remaining cream mixture. Spoon the mixture into the cavity of the cake.

Cover the chocolate cream mixture with pound cake and trim off any protruding pieces. Pull over the cheesecloth to cover and cover the bowl tightly with plastic wrap.

Refrigerate overnight or make 2 to 3 days ahead.

Unmold onto a serving dish. Remove cheesecloth and decorate with sifted confectioners' sugar and cocoa powder.

Diana Albanese

SALLY KOFKE studied Italian cooking with Marcella Hazan. She is a certified teacher and food professional through the IACP.

NICHOLAS MALGIERI, a Culinary Institute of America graduate, is the former executive pastry chef of Windows on the World. A nationally known teacher, his classes are sell-outs throughout the country. His two recent dessert cookbooks have garnered rave reviews.

Pleasures of Tuscany

Sally Kofke

Nicholas Malgieri

Pasta with Basil and Pignolia

Grilled Mushrooms and Radicchio (LEFT)

Chicken Breasts with Lemon and Sage (ABOVE)

Mango Macadamia Cake

Pasta with Basil and Pignolia

Serves 6

2 tablespoons extra-virgin olive oil

3 to 5 cloves garlic, peeled and minced

3 small firm zucchinis, washed, trimmed, and cut in 2" julienne

2 cups lightly packed basil leaves, shredded

1 pound spaghettini

1 cup freshly grated Parmigiano Reggiano

Salt and pepper to taste

⅓ cup pignolia, lightly toasted

In a medium sauté pan, heat the oil and gently cook the garlic until it just begins to color. Add the zucchini and cook, tossing, for several minutes until it is softened. Remove from the heat and stir in the shredded basil, reserving some for garnish.

Meanwhile, cook the pasta in 4 quarts of rapidly boiling, salted water until al dente. Drain, reserving some of the water and turn into a warm bowl.

Pour about ⅔ of the sauce and ½ cup of the Parmigiano Reggiano over the pasta and toss. Thin with a little of the reserved cooking water, if necessary.

Season to taste with salt and freshly ground pepper. Pour the rest of the sauce on top and lightly mix. Sprinkle with the reserved basil leaves and the pignolia and serve immediately on warm plates.

Pass the remaining cheese.

Sally Kofke

Grilled Mushrooms and Radicchio

Serves 6

3 radicchio, halved

1 large or 2 medium portobella mushrooms

Extra-virgin olive oil

Salt and pepper to taste

Preheat broiler or grill.

Trim the radicchio and remove any outer damaged leaves. Cut in half through the core.

Brush or wipe off the mushrooms and trim the ends of the stems. Cut the stems off so that the underside of the mushrooms can lie flat.

Spray a baking sheet lightly with cooking spray. Spread out the radicchio and mushrooms on the baking sheet and brush lightly with oil.

Place about 4 inches from the heat or directly on grill and cook about 10 minutes, turning frequently and brushing with oil when you turn the first time.

Season with salt and pepper to taste and serve.

Sally Kofke

Chicken Breasts with Lemon and Sage

Serves 6

Preheat oven to 350°F.

Place the seasoned flour in a medium bowl. Lightly dust the chicken with the flour, brushing off any excess. Whisk the broth into the remaining flour and set aside.

Meanwhile, heat the oil in a skillet or sauté pan large enough to hold the chicken in a single layer. When hot, add the chicken pieces and sauté until golden brown. Pour out any remaining fat and whisk in the chicken stock and flour mixture and the lemon zest.

Cover and place in the preheated oven. Cook about 15 to 20 minutes, or until the chicken is just done.

Remove the chicken with a slotted spoon to a warm platter, cover and keep warm.

Mix together the egg yolks and lemon juice and whisk into the pan sauces. Place over medium heat and whisk constantly until hot and thickened. Do not boil!

Season to taste with salt and pepper and mix in the minced sage.

Mix in any juices from the chicken and spoon some of the sauce over the chicken. Pass the rest separately.

Sally Kofke

3 tablespoons flour, seasoned with salt and pepper and a pinch of red pepper

3 whole boneless chicken breasts, skinned and cut in half

1½ cups chicken broth

Olive oil

Finely grated zest of one lemon

3 egg yolks

3 tablespoons lemon juice

Salt and freshly ground pepper to taste

3 tablespoons fresh sage, minced

Lemon slices and sprigs of fresh sage for garnish

The lemon and sage in this chicken dish complement the flavors of grilled mushrooms and radicchio. If the radicchio is very large, quarter it before cooking.

Mango Macadamia Cake

Except for the egg yolks in the cake batter, this is a virtually fat-free cake, making it much more appealing for warm weather.

MACADAMIA CAKE LAYER

4 eggs, separated

½ cup sugar, divided

Pinch salt

1 cup Macadamia nuts, rinsed, lightly toasted and ground in the food processor

⅔ cup cake flour

½ cup Macadamias, rinsed, coarsely chopped and toasted

MANGO FILLING

4 large, ripe mangoes

3 tablespoons sugar

2 tablespoons water

LIME AND RUM SAUCE

Juice of 1 lime and zest

½ cup sugar

3 tablespoons water

1 tablespoon butter

2 tablespoons dark rum

For the cake layer, butter a 10-inch round cake pan and line the bottom with a piece of parchment or waxed paper cut to fit. Whip the yolks with half the sugar until very light, about 5 minutes. With clean bowl and beater(s) whip the egg whites with the salt until white and opaque. Whip in the remaining sugar gradually, continuing to whip until the whites hold a firm peak.

Fold the yolks into the whites, then fold in the ground Macadamias. Sift the cake flour over the batter and fold it in. Pour the batter into the prepared pan and bake at 350°F., about 30 minutes, until well risen and firm. Unmold and cool the layer on a rack.

For the filling, peel, slice, and seed the mangoes. Cut the mango flesh into ½ inch wide strips. Place the sugar in a medium saucepan and stir in a few drops of water. Place over low heat and allow to melt and caramelize. When the sugar is a deep amber color, add the remaining water (carefully and at arm's length), then the mango strips. Return to a boil and cool.

For the sauce, caramelize sugar as in the filling, and add water, butter, lime juice and zest, and rum. Drain filling and add juices to sauce.

To assemble cake, split layer in half and place on platter. Top first layer with half the filling. Place second layer on cake and top with remaining filling, arranging it as neatly as possible. Sprinkle top of filling with the toasted, chopped macadamias. When serving cake, top each portion with a spoonful of sauce.

Nick Malgieri

STEVEN CAPODICASA, a graduate of the Culinary Institute of America, cooked for several U.S. presidents while working for the Hilton Hotel chain. Steve was head of new product development for Kings Super Markets. He presently serves on the advisory boards of numerous major food companies.

Couples: Summer Party Buffet

Steven Capodicasa

Grilled Oysters Casino

Roasted Orzo and Summer Grilled Vegetables (LEFT)

Grilled Lemon Peppercorn Tuna Steaks (ABOVE)

Baby Lettuce Served with a Roasted Yellow Pepper Vinaigrette

Homemade Peach and Grand Marnier Ice Cream

Grilled Summer Fruits with Vanilla Sauce

Grilled Oysters Casino

18 fresh large oysters

½ pound bacon cut into small ¼ inch dice

1 cup green peppers, diced finely

1 cup red peppers, diced finely

2 cloves garlic, minced

1 small onion, finely diced

¼ cup sweet sherry

Salt and pepper to taste

Choose oysters with tightly closed shells. Reject any that don't snap shut when tapped. Use them as soon as you can after purchasing, but they can be kept refrigerated, larger shell down and covered with a damp towel, for up to three days. You can have your fish monger open them for you if you like. Shucked, they will keep for two days.

Heat a large sauté pan. Add in diced bacon and slowly cook until the fat is rendered out and bacon is golden brown. Remove cooked bacon, reserving bacon fat in pan.

Sauté diced onion in hot bacon fat and simmer until onions get tender. Add in diced peppers and garlic. Continue to cook for 3 to 4 minutes. Add sherry to the skillet. Simmer and scrape the pan to deglaze. Add cooked bacon to cooked pepper mixture. Adjust seasonings with salt and pepper. Chill.

Carefully open oysters, saving oyster liquid. Add reserved liquid to bacon and vegetable mixture. Preheat broiler to high. Spoon bacon mixture over oysters and place under broiler. Cook for 3 minutes. Serve immediately.

Steven Capodicasa

Roasted Orzo and Summer Grilled Vegetables

Serves 6

Roast uncooked orzo in a preheated 350°F. oven until golden brown. Remove and cool.

Cook roasted orzo in salted boiling water, drain and hold.

Preheat grill on high. Toss sliced eggplant, peppers, and scallions with ¼ cup olive oil. Grill vegetables until tender. Chill.

Whisk together canola oil, red wine vinegar, mashed garlic, pignolia nuts, and chopped parsley. Adjust seasoning with salt and pepper. Toss with cooked orzo.

Coarsely chop grilled vegetables and add to cooked orzo.

Steven Capodicasa

1 pound orzo

1 pound baby Japanese eggplants, sliced

1 red pepper sliced into quarters

1 yellow pepper sliced into quarters

2 scallions sliced on 1-inch bias

2 cloves roasted garlic, mashed

¼ cup olive oil

½ cup canola oil

¼ cup red wine vinegar

½ cup pignolia nuts, toasted

¼ cup parsley, chopped

Salt and pepper to taste

Grilled Lemon Peppercorn Tuna Steaks

Serves 6

Six each ¾ inch thick fresh tuna steaks

Zest of 2 lemons

Juice of 2 lemons

¼ cup whole peppercorns, coarsely crushed

¼ cup olive oil

¼ cup fresh dill, chopped

Kosher salt to taste

¼ cup light soy sauce

This dish is a fabulous takeoff on a steak au poivre. Crush the peppercorns in a plastic bag with the bottom of a cast-iron skillet or a flat meat mallet. Buy a good quality tuna and serve this dish rare.

Mix crushed peppercorns, chopped dill, and Kosher salt in a bowl. Sprinkle on both sides of tuna steaks and gently press into each steak.

To prepare the marinade, mix together olive oil, zest, and lemon juice in a non-reactive dish. Place seasoned tuna steaks in marinade for 1 hour under refrigeration.

Heat grill on high and lightly oil grids of grill. Grill seasoned tuna steaks on each side for 2 to 3 minutes for rare and 4 to 5 minutes on each side for medium. Discard marinade.

Remove from grill. Toss with light soy sauce.

Steven Capodicasa

Baby Lettuce Served with a Roasted Yellow Pepper Vinaigrette

Serves 6 to 8

18 ounces fresh baby lettuce

6 large yellow peppers

½ cup olive oil

4 sprigs fresh thyme, chopped

1 clove garlic, peeled

Salt

Pepper

⅓ cup fresh lemon juice

1 tablespoon fresh lemon zest

2 Kirby cucumbers, sliced thin

1 small red onion, sliced thin

Place yellow peppers over an open flame, char until black, and place in a brown paper bag and seal. After 15 to 20 minutes take peppers from bag and remove blackened skin and seeds.

Arrange baby greens on a platter and garnish with cucumbers and onions.

Place roasted peppers in a blender with canola oil, half of lemon juice, garlic, chopped thyme, and zest, process.

Adjust seasonings with salt, pepper, and reserved lemon juice if needed.

Steven Capodicasa

Homemade Peach and Grand Marnier Ice Cream

Serves 8

Split vanilla bean in half. Gently scrape out seeds and add pod and seeds to heavy cream. Stir in half of sugar. Bring mixture to a simmer until sugar dissolves. Remove vanilla pods from cream and seeds and refrigerate.

Place chopped peaches in a saucepan. Stir in balance of sugar and Grand Marnier; cook slowly. Simmer sugar and peaches for 5 minutes until peaches are tender. Refrigerate until cool.

Mix cooked peaches and sweetened cream together. Adjust seasonings with a pinch of salt.

Follow directions from ice-cream maker.

Serve with a few drops of balsamic vinegar.

Steven Capodicasa

2 vanilla beans

1 quart heavy cream

¾ cup sugar

¼ cup Grand Marnier

2 cups peaches, chopped and pitted

Balsamic vinegar

Pinch of salt

Grilled Summer Fruits with Vanilla Sauce

6 ripe peaches, cut in half and pitted

6 ripe apricots, cut in half and pitted

6 ripe plums, cut in half and pitted

1 ripe cantaloupe, seeds removed and sliced into 8 wedges

1 ripe honeydew melon, seeds removed and sliced into 8 wedges

2 pints blueberries

2 pints strawberries

2 sticks unsalted butter, melted

½ cup sugar

Cinnamon

Mint for garnish

VANILLA SAUCE

1 pint light cream

2 vanilla beans, split and scraped

½ cup sugar

6 egg yolks

Pinch of salt

Combine cream, vanilla beans, and half of the sugar in a pot and heat the mixture to a boil.

Blend remaining sugar with the egg yolks until smooth. Temper this mixture with the heated cream; return the tempered yolks to the cream mixture.

Cook sauce over low heat, stirring constantly, until it coats the back of a wooden spoon.

Strain through a fine sieve and chill in an ice bath. Flavor vanilla sauce with any of your favorite liquers.

Preheat grill on high. Lightly brush melon wedges with melted butter and sprinkle with sugar. Grill on both sides for 2 to 6 minutes. Remove from grill and place on platter.

Lightly brush peaches, apricots, and plums with melted butter and sprinkle with sugar. Grill on both sides until soft. Remove from grill and add to the platter.

Place strawberries and blueberries into a bowl. Add remaining butter and sugar and toss to coat. (If using an outdoor grill, place a sheet of foil on grids.) Grill strawberries and blueberries on hot grill for 2 to 3 minutes. Remove from grill and add to platter.

Cut melon slices into bite-size pieces and toss all the fruits together. Drizzle with vanilla sauce and garnish with mint and cinnamon.

Steven Capodicasa

DIANA ALBANESE comes from a family that has owned a food market in Bayonne, NJ, for 75 years. She has been a private caterer and was director of La Cucina D'ana. Diana has studied at the French Culinary Institute and La Technique, and is on the faculty of Brookdale Community College's Creative Cooking Classes.

CAROLE WALTER, Certified Culinary Professional, is author of *Great Cakes*, a James Beard Award-winning cookbook. A consultant and teacher, she has appeared on many major network television shows. Carole has studied patisserie and culinary arts in Austria, Denmark, France, and Italy.

Cooking Al Fresco

Diana Albanese

Carole Walter

Grilled Boneless Leg of Lamb with Mint Pesto (ABOVE)

Grilled Potato and Rosemary Salad

Grilled Stuffed Eggplant Slices (LEFT)

Chocolate Fleck Layer Cake

Grilled Boneless Leg of Lamb with Mint Pesto

Serves 8

Two 3½-to-4-pound boneless, butterflied leg of lamb butt halves

MINT PESTO MARINADE

1 cup mint leaves

2 large garlic cloves

1 piece of ginger, about the same size as the garlic

3 tablespoons red pepper jelly

½ cup soy sauce

3 tablespoons vegetable oil

Boneless leg of lamb is perfect for the grill. To make the leg of lamb easier to handle, skewer each one flat with two metal skewers going diagonally in an "X" shape. Make sure to serve it pink.

Place mint, garlic, ginger, jelly, soy sauce, and vegetable oil in food processor. Process until puréed. Transfer to a large plastic bag.

Remove as much fat from the lamb as possible. Add lamb to bag and refrigerate for at least 2 hours or overnight. Turn 2 to 3 times.

Preheat outdoor grill to medium high heat, 400°F. For cooking indoors, adjust broiler rack to second rack from the top and preheat broiler.

Wipe the meat with paper towels and place directly on the grill. Grill on each side for approximately 7 to 8 minutes.

For cooking indoors, broil lamb for the same time. Using an instant-read thermometer, the internal temperature should be around 130°F. If not, place in a 350°F. oven until the meat registers that temperature. Let meat rest for 10 minutes.

Diana Albanese

48

Grilled Potato and Rosemary Salad

Serves 8

Preheat grill to 350°F. to 400°F. (medium heat).

In a small saucepan, heat the oil and three rosemary sprigs. When the rosemary starts to sizzle, shut off the heat and steep for half an hour. Discard rosemary.

Cut six pieces of heavy-duty foil that you can wrap each potato in.

Slice potatoes into ¼-inch rounds. Brush rosemary oil over slices. Place each potato on foil and sprinkle ½ tablespoon of chicken bouillon over and in between potato slices. Place a sprig of fresh rosemary and some rosemary oil on top. Wrap each potato in foil.

Cook potatoes on the grill for 35 to 40 minutes or until tender, turning halfway through. To cook indoors, bake in a preheated 400°F. oven on a sheetpan on the bottom rack for the same length of time.

In a large bowl, combine sun-dried tomatoes, olives, scallions, garlic, and parsley. Unwrap cooked potatoes and discard rosemary. Add potatoes to salad bowl, separating slices.

In a bowl, combine mustard and vinegar. Whisk in remaining rosemary oil and season with salt and pepper. Pour dressing over potato salad and serve warm.

Diana Albanese

¾ cup olive oil

Bunch of fresh rosemary

6 baking potatoes, about ½ pound each, scrubbed

Salt and freshly ground black pepper

3 tablespoons instant seasoned chicken bouillon

½ cup sun-dried tomatoes in oil, julienned

10 Calamata olives, pitted and sliced

1 bunch scallions, chopped

1 teaspoon garlic, minced

2 tablespoons parsley, snipped

1 teaspoon Dijon mustard

2 tablespoons sherry wine vinegar

Grilled Stuffed Eggplant Slices

2 eggplants, 1¼ pounds each

¾ cup olive oil, seasoned with salt and pepper

1 medium onion, chopped

One 14½-ounce can fresh cut tomatoes

Pinch of sugar

1 sprig of fresh basil

¼ cup Parmesan cheese, grated

1 egg yolk, beaten lightly

1 tablespoon wine vinegar

Basil leaves for garnish

Assemble the grilled eggplant slices ahead of time and heat them through before serving. You may have to add a few more minutes of baking time if the eggplant slices started out cold.

Trim eggplant and slice into ¾- to 1-inch rounds. You should have 20 to 22 slices.

Preheat outdoor grill to medium heat or indoor grill pan to medium heat. Brush eggplant rounds with seasoned olive oil and cook for 10 minutes on each side.

While the eggplant is cooking, start the tomato mixture. Heat 3 tablespoons of seasoned oil on medium heat in a saucepan. Add chopped onions and sauté for 6 to 7 minutes. Add tomatoes, pinch of sugar, and sprig of basil.

Cook for 20 minutes or until mixture is thick and pulpy. Remove basil and set aside to cool.

As soon as the eggplant is cooked, place on a lightly oiled sheet pan. Preheat oven to 400°F.

Combine grated cheese, egg yolk, and vinegar with tomatoes. Top half of the eggplants with tomato mixture and place remaining eggplant slices on top. Heat through in oven for 10 minutes. Garnish with basil.

Diana Albanese

Chocolate Fleck Layer Cake

Serves 10 to 12

Preheat oven to 350°F. Place shelf in lower third of oven. Butter the bottom and sides of two 9-inch layer pans. Line the bottoms with circles of buttered baking parchment or waxed paper.

Cut the chocolate into pieces. Place in a food processor fitted with the steel blade. Pulse to break into smaller pieces, then process until finely chopped.

Strain the flour, baking powder, and salt together 3 times. Set aside.

Place butter into the large bowl of an electric mixer fitted with beaters or paddle attachment. Soften on low speed. Increase speed to medium. Cream until light in color, about 2 minutes.

Add the sugar 1 tablespoon at a time over 6 to 8 minutes. Scrape sides of bowl as needed. Add eggs, 1 at a time at 1-minute intervals. Blend in vanilla.

Reduce speed to low. Add flour mixture alternately with milk, dividing the dry ingredients into 3 parts and liquid into 2 parts. Add the chopped chocolate and mix just to blend, about 10 seconds longer.

Empty the batter into the prepared pans. Smooth surface.

Bake for 25 to 30 minutes or until the cakes are golden brown on the surface and the sides begin to release from the pan.

Remove from the oven and place on cake racks to cool. After 10 minutes, invert onto racks and remove pans and paper.

Carole Walter

2¼ cups sifted cake flour

2¼ teaspoons baking powder

½ teaspoon salt

¾ cup unsalted butter, cool but not cold

1⅓ cups superfine sugar

3 large eggs

1 teaspoon vanilla extract

¾ cup milk

2 ounces bittersweet chocolate, fine quality

Creamy Chocolate Frosting

8 ounces bittersweet
chocolate, fine quality

1 cup (2 sticks) unsalted butter

¾ cup pasteurized eggs

1½ teaspoons vanilla extract

This recipe provides enough to fill and cover the top and sides of two 9-inch layers.

In the top of a double boiler, melt the chocolate with the butter *very* slowly. Blend gently with a wire whisk until smooth.

Whip the pasteurized eggs well in an electric mixer. Slowly add the chocolate mixture and beat until smooth (about 1 minute). Blend in the vanilla.

Chill in the refrigerator until thick and creamy, about 1 hour. Stir occasionally. If the icing becomes too cold, let it stand at room temperature until soft enough to spread.

To assemble the cake, place the most even layer top-side down onto a cake plate. Spread with frosting to ½ inch from the outer edge of the cake.

Arrange the second layer top-side up. Using an icing spreader, coat the sides of the cake with frosting. Then cover the top. Spread the remaining frosting around the sides. To create a pretty swirled effect, when the cake is completed, move the bottom of a tablespoon over the frosting, sweeping the icing into graceful curves.

Carole Walter

WADE BURCH attended the School for American Chefs at Beringer Vineyards in Napa Valley, CA, with Madeleine Kamman. Wade was Executive Sous Chef at The Plaza Hotel in New York and former executive chef at the Grand Summit Hotel. He is a certified chef de cuisine, and has worked with such noted chefs as Stephan Pyles (Baby Routh, Dallas) and with Larry Forgione of Manhattan Prime.

Memorial Day Barbecue

Wade Burch

Molasses Barbecued Chicken (ABOVE)

Jicama Cole Slaw

Cowboy Ranch Beans

Nancy's Peach Cobbler (LEFT)

Molasses Barbecued Chicken

Serves 8

Two each 2½-to-3-pound whole chickens cut into quarters

BBQ SAUCE

2 yellow onions, minced

2 jalapeño peppers, seeded, minced

2 garlic cloves, minced

2 teaspoons canola oil

1 cup brown sugar

2 cups molasses

3 tablespoons yellow mustard

3 cups ketchup

2 teaspoons Worcestershire sauce

2 teaspoons salt

1 teaspoon black pepper, coarsely ground

Preheat grill so it is nice and hot on medium heat.

Heat a sauté pan over high heat. Add the oil and sauté the peppers, onions, and garlic for three minutes.

Add the remaining ingredients and cook five minutes more.

Lower the heat and simmer for 15 to 20 minutes.

Grill the chicken skin-side-down for 8 to 10 minutes. Turn the chicken over and brush liberally with the sauce. Baste the chicken with sauce every 5 to 7 minutes until the chicken is cooked through.

Wade Burch

Make this barbecue sauce ahead of time. When handling hot peppers, first coat your hands lightly with any kind of cooking oil. When you are finished, wash your hands—the oils from the peppers will wash off with the cooking oil. To reduce the heat of any chili pepper, remove more of the seeds and veins. Make sure your grill is very hot before you start the chicken. And don't poke it with a fork! You'll let out all the juices.

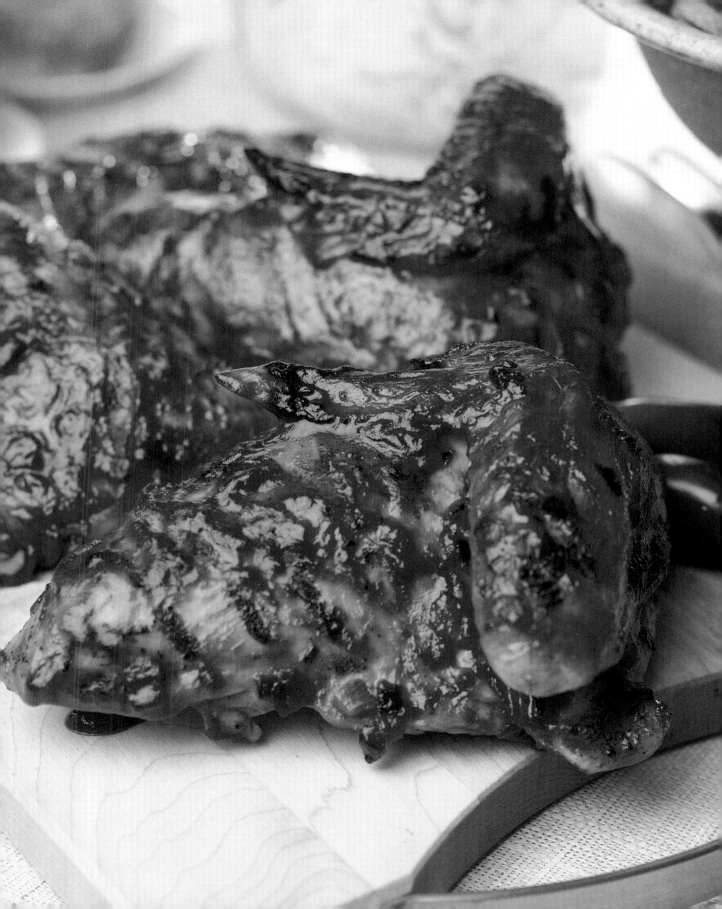

Jicama Cole Slaw

2 jicamas, peeled, julienned

1 head cabbage, julienned

1 red bell pepper, julienned

2 carrots, julienned

SLAW DRESSING

2 cups mayonnaise

1/4 cup sour cream

2 teaspoons cider vinegar

1/2 teaspoon dry mustard

1/2 teaspoon Tabasco

1/2 teaspoon chili powder

1 teaspoon salt

1/2 teaspoon black pepper

1/2 teaspoon cumin, ground

2 tablespoons sugar

Combine the dressing ingredients in a bowl with a whisk.

Toss the vegetables with the dressing to coat thoroughly.

Refrigerate until needed.

Wade Burch

Cowboy Ranch Beans

Serves 8

Soak the beans in water for at least 2 hours or overnight.

Heat a medium saucepan over high heat. Sauté the onion and pepper in the oil for three minutes. Add the garlic and jalapeño and cook two minutes more.

Add the drained beans, tomatoes, and stock. Bring to a boil.

Tie the herbs and spices in a cheesecloth to form a bag. Add it to the pot.

Lower the heat to a simmer and cook for 1 hour, stirring occasionally, until the beans are soft.

Remove the sachet bag.

Add the remaining ingredients. Keep warm until ready to serve.

Wade Burch

1 cup pinto beans, picked clean

2 tablespoons canola oil

1 yellow onion, medium dice

1 green bell pepper, seeded, small dice

2 garlic cloves, minced

1 jalapeno pepper, minced

2 tomatoes, peeled, seeded, diced

4 cups chicken stock

$\frac{1}{2}$ teaspoon ground cumin

$\frac{1}{2}$ teaspoon ground coriander

$\frac{1}{2}$ teaspoon ground chili powder

$\frac{1}{2}$ bay leaf

3 thyme sprigs

1 teaspoon black peppercorns

1 red bell pepper, roasted, peeled, seeded, diced

1 green bell pepper, roasted, peeled, seeded, diced

1 yellow bell pepper, roasted, peeled, seeded, diced

1 bunch cilantro, washed, chopped

2 tablespoons salt

Tabasco to taste

Nancy's Peach Cobbler

Serves 8

1 cup flour

1 cup sugar

1 cup milk

3 teaspoons baking powder

1 stick butter

1 quart peaches, sliced

Preheat the oven to 350°F.

Combine the dry ingredients in a bowl.

Stir the milk into the bowl slowly.

Melt the butter in a 9 × 11-inch baking dish. Add the fruit and heat in the oven for 5 minutes.

Remove from the oven and pour the batter over the fruit. Return to oven.

Bake for 30 to 40 minutes or until golden brown.

Serve in a bowl and top with vanilla ice cream.

Wade Burch

FALL

MICHAEL SALVATORE is a graduate of the Academy of Culinary Arts who has been cooking since age three at his grandmother's knee. He served as executive chef for Hyatt Hotels and has owned two restaurants. He now teaches cooking in the U.S. and France.

Feast of San Gennaro

Michael Salvatore

Italian Sausage with Peppers and Onions (FACING PAGE)

Fried Calamari (LEFT)

Nana's Marinara Sauce

Zeppole (ABOVE)

Italian Sausage with Peppers and Onions

1½ pounds pork butt, cubed

Kosher salt and black pepper to taste

1 teaspoon hot Hungarian paprika

1 teaspoon ground coriander

3 teaspoons whole fennel seeds

1 teaspoon dextrose

Crushed red pepper to taste

2 ounces Parmegiano Reggiano

6 ounces Caciocavallo

1 tablespoon Italian parsley, chopped

2 ounces red wine

Natural casings, rinsed, as needed

2 green bell peppers

2 yellow onions

3 tablespoons garlic, minced

4 fresh Italian torpedo rolls

6 ounces extra-virgin olive oil

If you can't go to the Feast of San Gennaro, create your own! Master the art of making your own sausage, then vary the ingredients any way you like.

To make the sausages, grate the cheeses together and reserve. Mix together the dextrose, salt, pepper, fennel, coriander, hot pepper, and paprika. Mix well with the meat.

Grind meat mixture through a medium die. Mix in cheeses and parsley using a paddle until evenly textured. Test and adjust seasonings.

Thread the casings onto the tube and begin to fill the casings. Reserve, chilled until service.

To make the sandwiches, on a griddle over medium heat, add 3 ounces of olive oil and place a loop of sausage on griddle. Cook about 5 to 7 minutes per side.

Before turning the sausage, begin the vegetables. Sauté the onions and green peppers until golden in the olive oil. Fold in the garlic and move to the coolest place on the griddle. Cut the rolls lengthwise; place them open on top on the cooked vegetables to warm through. Cut the cooked sausage into 4 equal links and stuff into the sandwiches.

NOTE: Add tomato sauce, hot peppers, and cheeses of your choice, if desired.

Michael Salvatore

Fried Calamari

Check the squid to ensure that they are properly cleaned; that is, no wings or "bone" on or in the tubes, no beak or stomach attached to the tentacles. Cut tubes into rings.

Heat oil to 350°F. Combine cornstarch and flour; add cracked black pepper, salt, and half the parsley. Mix well.

Dredge the calamari in the seasoned flour mixture, shake off the excess, and begin frying in small batches so that the oil does not lose temperature. Cook until almost golden (less than 1 minute), remove, and drain.

Sprinkle with remaining parsley and serve immediately with marinara sauce and lemon wedges.

Michael Salvatore

2 pounds cleaned squid, tubes and tentacles

8 ounces flour

8 ounces cornstarch

2 tablespoons cracked black pepper

2 tablespoons Kosher salt

4 tablespoons Italian parsley, chopped

2 lemons, quartered

2 quarts oil for frying

1 pint marinara sauce

Don't overcook the calamari. Cooking calamari too long makes it rubbery.

Nana's Marinara Sauce

Makes 2 Quarts

Place the tomatoes in small batches in a food processor and pulse until chunky.

In a heavy stockpot over medium-high heat, heat the olive oil with the bay leaves. Add the onions and sauté until almost golden, stir in the garlic. Do not brown. Add the tomatoes and reduce to medium heat. Bring to simmer, stirring frequently.

Taste for acidity. If tomatoes are too sour, add enough sugar so that they are balanced in flavor, but not sweet.

Simmer 10 to 15 minutes, season with salt and pepper. Remove from heat and stir in the fresh herbs.

Michael Salvatore

4 pounds Roma tomatoes, peeled

12 ounces yellow onions, diced

3 ounces garlic, minced

2 bay leaves

¼ cup fresh basil, chopped

2 tablespoons fresh oregano, chopped

Kosher salt to taste

Freshly ground black pepper to taste

Granulated sugar, only if necessary

Crushed red pepper to taste (optional)

4 ounces extra-virgin olive oil

Zeppole

Makes 20 Doughnuts

4 cups flour

1½ tablespoons fresh yeast

1 cup milk, lukewarm

2 small eggs

2½ ounces granulated sugar

1 teaspoon lemon zest, grated

Pinch of Kosher salt

3 tablespoons butter, melted

Frying oil as needed

Confectioners' sugar as needed

Combine the yeast and milk and set aside to proof for 2 minutes. Sift the flour into a bowl and make a well. Add the milk mixture, slowly, to the flour and work to a smooth dough. Cover with a kitchen towel and set aside to rise for roughly 2 hours or until doubled in volume.

Beat together the eggs, sugar, salt, and zest. Punch down dough and add the egg mixture; knead smooth. Add the melted butter gradually. The dough will be sticky at this point. Continue kneading until cooled and smooth again. Roll out no thinner than a ¼-inch thick and, using a biscuit cutter, cut into 2-inch circles. Spread the cut dough out and allow to rise, covered, until doubled again.

Deep fry at 350°F. until golden in batches so as not to cool the oil. Remove and drain excess oil. Coat liberally with the confectioners' sugar and serve immediately.

Michael Salvatore

DEB BARRETT is a professional baker, private chef, and caterer.
KATHIE FINN graduated from Peter Kump's professional program with a Blue Ribbon diploma. Following an apprenticeship in corporate dining, she has worked as a private chef and caterer.

Thanksgiving Dinner

Deb Barrett

Kathie Finn

Wild Mushroom Soup

Pears, Pecans, and Blue Cheese with Fresh Cranberry Vinaigrette

Butterflied Roast Turkey

Apple, Sausage, and Leek Stuffing (ABOVE)

Herbed Potato and Butternut Squash Gratin (LEFT)

Pumpkin Crème Brûlée

Wild Mushroom Soup

Serves 6

1 ounce dried porcini mushrooms

3½ ounces oyster mushrooms

3½ ounces shiitake mushrooms

10 ounces cremini mushrooms

10 ounces white mushrooms

2 tablespoons olive oil

¼ cup sherry

6 cups chicken stock

1 cup demi glace

¼ cup snipped chives

Place the porcini mushrooms in a 2-cup measure and add 1 cup boiling water. Cover loosely and set aside for 10 to 15 minutes. Reserve the soaking liquid when you drain the mushrooms. Rinse the mushrooms well and chop coarsely. Pass the soaking liquid through a fine sieve, or strainer lined with a paper towel and reserve.

While the porcini are soaking, slice the oyster mushrooms and set aside. Wipe the shiitake, cremini, and white mushrooms carefully with paper towels, remove the stems, and cut into generous ¼-inch thick slices.

Heat a 6-quart stockpot over medium heat and add the olive oil, swirling to coat. Add all of the mushrooms, except the porcini, and mix gently to coat with the oil. Sauté the mushrooms over medium heat for about 10 to 15 minutes, or until they have given up their liquid and are beginning to brown. (Note: The more the mushrooms cook, the more flavorful the soup will be.)

Add the sherry and scrape the bottom of the pan to release any browned bits. Add the diced porcini mushrooms, then stir in the 6 cups of chicken stock. Continue to cook over low heat.

Bring the strained porcini liquid to a simmer and add the demi glace. Remove from the heat and stir to dissolve. Add to the soup, stirring gently. If serving immediately, bring the soup to a slow boil, then ladle into warmed serving bowls and garnish with the snipped chives.

DO AHEAD: Soup may be refrigerated up to 3 days. Garnish with chives before service.

Kathie Finn

Pears, Pecans, and Blue Cheese with Fresh Cranberry Vinaigrette

Serves 10

Cranberry Vinaigrette

Place all of the ingredients in a blender and mix until emulsified. Taste for seasoning. Set the vinaigrette aside for an hour to allow the flavors to blend.

½ pound fresh cranberries, washed and picked over

¼ cup cranberry juice

1 tablespoon Dijon mustard

1 tablespoon maple syrup

1 tablespoon shallot, chopped

2 tablespoons fresh lime juice

2 tablespoons raspberry vinegar

½ teaspoon kosher salt

⅛ teaspoon black pepper

¼ cup vegetable oil

Salad

Wash and dry the greens carefully and tear into bite-size pieces. Roll in paper towels and store in the refrigerator until ready to use.

Melt the butter in a sauté pan and toast the pecans in the butter until brown and fragrant. Toss with salt and pepper. Allow the nuts to cool completely before using.

Toss the greens with a small amount of the vinaigrette and arrange on individual plates. Mound the julienned pear slices on top of the greens and drizzle with the vinaigrette. Garnish with the toasted pecans and crumbled cheese. Serve immediately.

Deb Barrett

4 Asian pears, washed, sliced, and julienned

1 head frisee or chickory

2 bunches baby arugula

1 bunch watercress

1 cup whole pecans

½ pound blue cheese, crumbled

1 tablespoon unsalted butter

Kosher salt and freshly ground black pepper

Butterflied Roast Turkey

Serves 8 to 10

To brine a turkey, find a pot just large enough to accommodate the turkey. It can be an aluminum pot, because it will be lined with a plastic bag. Dissolve the sugar and salt in 1 quart of room temperature water. Add the rest of the water to make 2 gallons of solution. Add the peppercorn. Place the turkey in the lined pot and pour in the brine.

Gather up the bag and carefully squeeze out the air so that the turkey is completely covered with the liquid. Seal the bag with a twist tie and place the pot in the refrigerator or a place where the temperature will not go above 40°F. Allow the turkey to soak for 4 to 6 hours. (This can be done on the morning of the day it is to be roasted.)

After the allotted soaking time has elapsed, remove the turkey from the brine and place it on a baking sheet with sides to drip off. Blot the turkey with paper towels to dry the skin. Allow the turkey to reach room temperature uncovered.

To roast, adjust the oven rack to the lower third of the oven. Preheat the oven to 450°F. Have a low-sided roasting or baking pan with a rack ready.

Place the turkey skin-side-up on a large cutting board and cover it with plastic wrap. Lightly pound the flesh to conform it to a uniform thickness.

Place the turkey on the rack in the roasting or baking pan, skin-side-up. Tuck the wings under the bird and secure the legs to keep them from moving while roasting. Rub the skin with the soft butter and place the turkey in the oven. Pour about 2 cups of chicken broth into the bottom of the pan.

Close the door and roast for 10 minutes. Reduce the oven temperature to 400°F. Continue roasting for about 1 hour, or until a thermometer reads 175°F. when inserted into the thigh. You may need to add chicken stock to the bottom of the pan during roasting. Do not allow the meat juices to burn. Remove the turkey from the oven and transfer it to a cutting board. Allow the turkey to rest for 20 minutes tented with foil.

To make gravy, remove the fat from the pan juices. Set the pan juices aside.

Place the roasting pan over a burner. Over medium high heat, start scraping up the brown bits that have accumulated on the bottom of the pan. Sprinkle the flour over the pan and allow the flour to absorb the moisture. It will look like a brown paste.

BRINE

12-to-14-pound all natural turkey, thawed, backbone removed. (Reserve giblets and backbone for gravy.)

2 gallons water

2 cups Kosher salt

1 cup granulated sugar

1 teaspoon whole peppercorns

1 large heavy plastic bag

2 tablespoons unsalted butter, room temperature

1 quart chicken stock, homemade and unsalted if possible, or lowest sodium content possible

4 tablespoons flour (Wondra brand is best)

1 cup white wine

Fresh thyme sprigs

Make sure your turkey is moist by brining it first. This recipe removes the backbone and flattens the turkey, greatly reducing the baking time. Don't forget to let the turkey "rest" before carving it so that it can reabsorb the juices.

Cook this paste over medium low heat for 2 to 3 minutes to remove the raw taste of the flour. Add the wine and stir with a whisk to remove any lumps. Add the reserved pan drippings and any chicken stock you may have left. Add the thyme sprigs and simmer over medium low heat until the gravy has thickened. Taste carefully and season. Strain the gravy before serving.

With the reserved giblets and/or turkey back, a very flavorful stock can be made for the gravy. Chop the back into quarters and brown in a pan until golden. Add one stalk of celery, one carrot, and half a yellow onion. Add water or water and chicken broth to just cover. Bring to a boil and lower the heat to a simmer.

Simmer for at least 2 hours, skimming any scum and fat that rises to the top. Strain before using.

Deb Barrett

Apple, Sausage, and Leek Stuffing

Serves 8 to 10

3 cups chicken stock, divided

4 ounces (1 stick) unsalted butter, cut into 1-inch pieces

1 package prepared stuffing mix

2 large leeks, the white and part of the pale green

2 to 3 large apples (Golden Delicious, Rome, or Granny Smith)

1½ pounds bulk breakfast sausage, defrosted if frozen

1 teaspoon Kosher salt

Heat the oven to 350°F. Butter a 3-quart casserole *very* well. Set aside.

Heat 2½ cups of the chicken stock and butter, until the butter is melted. Place the stuffing mix in a large bowl and pour the liquid over it, stirring to combine.

Quarter the leeks lengthwise and rinse well under cold running water. Wipe dry with paper towels and cut into ½-inch slices. (Should make about 1½ cups.) Set aside.

Peel and core the apples and cut into ½-inch chunks. (Should make about 3½ cups.) Set aside.

Heat a 12-inch skillet over medium heat. Break the sausage into pieces and add to the skillet. Cook over medium heat until no traces of pink remain. Remove with a slotted spoon and set aside. A tablespoon or two of fat will remain in the skillet. (If not, add enough vegetable oil to equal 2 tablespoons.)

Sauté the leeks over low heat for 5 to 7 minutes, until wilted. Add to the sausage. Sauté the apple, adding more oil if necessary, until the pieces begin to caramelize. Deglaze the pan with ½ cup of the chicken stock. Add the apples and their liquid to the sausage-leek mixture.

Working in batches, pulse the sausage mixture in the work bowl of a food processor fitted with the steel blade, until it is coarsely chopped. Add to the stuffing 1 teaspoon of Kosher salt, blending well. Empty the stuffing into the prepared casserole.

Cover the stuffing with a piece of buttered aluminum foil and bake for 30 minutes, then uncover and bake for another 20 to 25 minutes to crisp the top. Let rest for 10 to 15 minutes before serving.

Kathie Finn

Herbed Potato and Butternut Squash Gratin

Serves 10

2½ to 3 pounds butternut squash, peeled

2½ pounds baking potatoes, peeled

1 large yellow onion, thinly sliced to measure (about 2 cups)

1 teaspoon sugar

3 tablespoons unsalted butter

1 tablespoon vegetable oil

1 tablespoon fresh thyme leaves

4 cups heavy cream

Kosher salt

Freshly ground pepper

1½ cups grated Asiago cheese

Have a buttered 9 × 13-inch ovenproof pan ready.

Heat a large sauté pan and add 1 tablespoon butter and 1 tablespoon oil. When butter has melted, add onions and toss to coat. Cover the pan with a lid and allow the onions to steam and collapse. This should take about 3 to 5 minutes. Remove the lid and stir the onions. Lower the heat slightly, add the 1 teaspoon of sugar and a pinch of salt. Allow the onions to cook, stirring occasionally, until they become a golden brown. Remove the pan from the heat and set aside.

Slice the potatoes and squash in a food processor fitted with a 2 mm. blade. Separate the vegetables.

Starting with the potatoes, layer the vegetables into the buttered pan. Season each layer with a sprinkling of Kosher salt and freshly ground pepper. Season every other layer with ⅓ of the thyme leaves and ½ of the onions. You should have 3 alternating layers. Continue until the pan is full.

Place the baking pan on a parchment- or foil-lined baking sheet. Pour the heavy cream over the vegetables. It should come ¾ up the side of the pan.

Cover with the grated cheese and bake at 400°F. for about one hour, or until the cream has been absorbed and the vegetables are very soft when tested with a knife. If the cheese starts to brown too much, cover the top loosely with buttered foil and continue baking. Allow the gratin to rest for 15 minutes before serving.

Deb Barrett

Pumpkin Crème Brûlée

Serves 10

Heat oven to 350°F. Have ready ten ½-cup custard cups, a baking pan (large enough to hold the cups) lined with 2 paper towels, and 1 quart boiling water.

Combine the half & half, sugar, allspice, cinnamon sticks, cloves, and ginger root. Heat *just* until boiling, then remove from the heat and let cool for 30 minutes.

In a large bowl, whisk the egg yolks and pumpkin puree until smooth. Strain the cooled half & half into the pumpkin mixture, whisking to thoroughly combine. (For ease of portioning, transfer the mixture to a liquid measuring cup.)

Place the custard cups in the prepared baking pan, then strain the custard into each cup, filling them just to the top. Place the pan on the oven rack, then add enough boiling water to come halfway up the sides of the cups. Bake for about 30 minutes. The sides should be set, but the centers should still be "jiggly."

Remove from the oven and carefully remove the cups from the baking pan. Chill for 2 to 3 hours to set. (May be prepared 1 day ahead up to this point.)

To glaze: Place the custard cups on a cookie sheet. Strain about 2 teaspoons of superfine sugar over the top of each custard. Using a propane torch or, alternatively, an oven broiler, heat the sugar until it is caramelized. Serve immediately.

NOTE: If using a broiler, place the cups in a baking pan, then place ice cubes around the cups. Fill the pan with water before placing under the broiler. This will help keep the custard cool so it does not curdle while the sugar is caramelizing.

Kathie Finn

1 quart half & half cream

⅔ cup sugar

10 to 12 whole allspice berries

2 cinnamon sticks

6 whole cloves

2-inch piece of fresh ginger, cut into ½-inch dice

10 large egg yolks, room temperature

1 cup canned pumpkin purée

½ cup superfine sugar

DANIEL C. ROSATI is owner of La Villa Cucina, a cooking school in the Tuscany region of Italy. He also teaches at the New School for Social Research in New York and various other schools around the country. His work with several noted chefs includes a position as teaching assistant to Giuliano Bugialli. A member of the IACP, Daniel's specialties include regional Italian cooking, Middle Eastern cooking, and pastry arts.

La Villa Cucina

Daniel C. Rosati

Focaccia with Tomato and Potato (LEFT)

Tagliatelle with Asparagus Sauce (OPPOSITE PAGE)

Vitello in Fricassea

Carciofi in Agro-Dolce (ABOVE)

Torta di Nocciole

Focaccia with Tomato and Potato

Serves 8 to 10

2 ounces fresh yeast or 3 packages active dry yeast

1¾ cups warm water

⅓ cup olive oil

4⅓ cups flour

1 teaspoon salt

2 tablespoons olive oil

⅓ cup olive oil

6 plum tomatoes, thinly sliced

6 red potatoes, cooked in boiling water until fork tender, cooled and thinly sliced

Additional olive oil for drizzling

2 teaspoons dry oregano

1 tablespoon Kosher salt

Place the yeast and water in the bowl of a stand mixer and whisk until well blended. Add the ⅓ cup olive oil, flour, and 1 teaspoon salt. Attach dough hook and blend until a smooth dough is achieved. Remove bowl from machine and cover with plastic wrap. Let dough stand in a warm area of the kitchen until doubled in bulk.

Lightly oil a 15 × 11-inch jelly-roll pan with 2 tablespoons of olive oil. Roll the dough just large enough to fit the pan; pat the dough to fill the pan completely. Cover lightly with plastic wrap. Place the dough in a warm area of the kitchen until doubled in size. Preheat oven to 350°F.

Remove plastic wrap from dough. Drizzle with remaining olive oil and gently spread around the surface of the dough. Dimple the surface of the dough with your fingertips at half-inch intervals making sure the tips of your fingers touch the bottom of the pan. Alternately arrange the slices of tomato and potato over surface of dough. Drizzle with olive oil. Sprinkle top with oregano and Kosher salt. Place dough in preheated oven and bake until golden. Serve warm.

Daniel C. Rosati

Tagliatelle with Asparagus Sauce

Serves 4 to 6

Trim off the dry woody bases of the asparagus, 1 inch from the bottom. Wash asparagus spears very well in several changes of water.

Cut the tips off the asparagus and reserve for later use.

Cut the remaining stems of the asparagus into ¼-inch pieces; place in a small pot with the garlic, water, ½ teaspoon salt, and pepper flakes. Place the pot over low heat and bring to a simmer; cover and allow asparagus pieces to cook until very tender. Add more water, if necessary, to keep moist.

With the aid of an immersion blender or food processor, puree cooked asparagus pieces until smooth. Add the olive oil and Parmigiano. Blend until smooth. Adjust seasoning, set aside until needed.

Bring the 8 quarts of water to a boil, add the Kosher salt, return to a boil. If fresh pasta is being used, add to water with the reserved asparagus tips, cook 4 minutes. If dry pasta is being used, cook according to package guidelines, adding the asparagus tips during the last 4 minutes of cooking.

Drain the cooked pasta, transfer to a serving bowl, toss with sauce. Drizzle with additional olive oil and garnish with additional parmigiano.

Daniel C. Rosati

2 pounds asparagus

4 cloves garlic

½ cup water

½ teaspoon salt

¼ teaspoon red pepper flakes

⅓ cup extra-virgin olive oil

½ cup grated Parmigiano

Salt

Pepper

8 quarts boiling water

2 tablespoons Kosher salt

1 pound tagliatelle fresh or dried

Don't get crazy looking for "tagliatelle" in the market. It's the northern Italian name for fettuccini.

Vitello in Fricassea
Fricassee of Veal

4 pounds veal cubes

¾ cup flour

½ cup olive oil

2 garlic cloves, minced

3 tablespoons fresh rosemary, minced

1 large red onion, minced

1 cup white wine

2 cups chicken stock

Salt, pepper

SAUCE

2 tablespoons olive oil

2 tablespoons butter

3 tablespoons flour

2 cups chicken stock, heated

4 egg yolks

2 lemons, juiced

Salt, pepper to taste

1 bunch Italian parsley, chopped

In a large casserole dish (preferably enamel), heat the ½ cup olive oil over medium heat. While oil is heating, quickly toss veal cubes in flour. Season well with salt and pepper. Place veal in casserole and cook until well browned on all sides. Lower heat and add the rosemary, onion, and garlic; cook until onions become transparent. Add wine and chicken stock. Simmer over low heat until meat is tender.

Remove veal from casserole with a slotted spoon, set aside until needed. Reduce cooking liquid by half, cooking uncovered over medium heat. In a medium saucepan, heat the butter and olive oil. Add the flour and stir over low heat 3 to 4 minutes. Add the heated chicken stock and stir until thick. Add the flour mixture to casserole and stir over low heat until well blended.

In a small bowl, combine the lemon juice and egg yolks. Season with salt and pepper, blend well. Slowly whisk lemon-egg mixture into casserole; whisk over low heat until thick. Return veal to casserole and heat thoroughly. Taste and adjust seasonings.

Place on a large serving platter. Spoon veal mixture onto center of plate, garnish with chopped parsley.

Daniel C. Rosati

Carciofi in Agro-Dolce
Sweet and Savory Marinated Artichokes

Arrange the artichokes, cut side up, in a casserole just large enough to hold them all in one layer.

Prepare the marinade: In a medium-size bowl combine the peppers, onion, garlic, red wine vinegar, balsamic vinegar, and honey. Whisk in the olive oil until well blended, then season well with salt and pepper.

Pour the marinade over the artichokes, garnish with thyme and parsley. Cover dish, refrigerate, and marinate at least 1 hour before serving or overnight.

Daniel C. Rosati

30 whole canned artichoke hearts, halved

MARINADE

1 red pepper, cut into tiny cubes

1 yellow pepper, cut into tiny cubes

1 red onion, minced

3 large garlic cloves, minced

Salt

Pepper

½ cup red wine vinegar

½ cup balsamic vinegar

1 tablespoon honey

1 cup extra-virgin olive oil

3 tablespoons fresh thyme, chopped

10 sprigs Italian parsley, leaves only, chopped

Torta di Nocciole
Chocolate Hazelnut Tart from Piedmont

NUT CRUST

1¾ cups all-purpose flour

½ cup hazelnuts, toasted, peeled, and finely ground

2 tablespoons cornstarch

¼ cup sugar

½ cup (1 stick) chilled unsalted butter, cut into small pieces

2 large eggs

1 teaspoon vanilla extract

FILLING

3 tablespoons unsalted butter, room temperature

½ cup sugar

2 large eggs

1 teaspoon vanilla extract

1¼ cups hazelnuts (about 7 ounces), toasted, peeled, and finely ground

2 tablespoons unsweetened cocoa powder

1 teaspoon baking powder

½ cup heavy cream

12 whole hazelnuts, toasted and peeled

GANACHE GLAZE

5 ounces bittersweet (not unsweetened) chocolate

½ cup heavy cream

To make the nut crust, combine flour, hazelnuts, cornstarch, and sugar in processor. Pulse 4 or 5 times or until mixture is well blended. Add butter and pulse 4 or 5 times or until mixture resembles coarse meal. Blend in eggs and vanilla; process until a ball of dough forms. Gather dough into a ball, flatten dough to form a disk, wrap in plastic wrap, and refrigerate 25 minutes.

Preheat oven to 375°F. Roll out dough on floured surface to 13-inch-diameter round. Transfer dough to 11-inch-diameter tart pan with removable bottom. Trim excess off edges. (For those who are apprehensive about rolling out dough, this dough can also be pressed into a tart pan.) Refrigerate until needed.

For the filling, use an electric mixer to beat the butter and sugar in a medium bowl until light and fluffy. Add eggs and vanilla, beat again until light and fluffy. In a small bowl, combine hazelnuts, cocoa, and baking powder. Stir until well blended. (If cocoa or baking powder is lumpy, sift through a fine strainer before blending.) Fold nut mixture into butter mixture alternately with cream. Pour mixture into prepared crust and bake for 30 to 40 minutes or until edges are well browned and center of torta springs back lightly when touched.

Transfer to rack. Allow torta to cool completely at room temperature before glazing.

To make the glaze, start by finely chopping chocolate in processor. Measure cream in glass measuring cup; microwave on high for about 1 minute or until very hot. With processor running, pour hot cream down feed tube, process until smooth. Pour ganache into small bowl, stir occasionally. Cool until thickened (about 10 minutes).

Spoon ganache into pastry bag fitted with small round tip. Drizzle the ganache from side to side over the surface of the torta. Turn the tart halfway around and repeat, creating lattice effect. Evenly space remaining hazelnuts around the inner edge.

Refrigerate torta until needed. Remove from refrigerator 20 minutes before serving, then transfer torta to decorative serving platter.

Daniel C. Rosati

HOLLY GUBER is former chef/owner of Terra Cotta restaurant in Maplewood, NJ. Holly continues to work as a private chef and consultant to several area caterers and restaurants.

An Elegant Fall Dinner

Holly Guber

Lemon Gnocchi with Crabmeat and Asparagus in Saffron Broth (LEFT)

Breast of Duck with Gingered Apricot Sauce (ABOVE)

Sweet Garlic Flan with Spring Herbs

Semifreddo Alle Mandorle

Lemon Gnocchi with Crabmeat and Asparagus in Saffron Broth

Serves 8

1 envelope active dry yeast

Pinch sugar

¼ cup warm water

2 cups flour

Salt and pepper

3 eggs, at room temperature

½ cup milk, warm

1 tablespoon olive oil

2 tablespoons chives, chopped

Grated zest of 1 lemon

2 tablespoons shallot, chopped

2 cups chicken stock

Generous pinch saffron

Hot red pepper flakes if desired (optional)

1 pound asparagus, trimmed and cut into 1-inch lengths

½ pound crabmeat, picked over

2 tablespoons butter

Finely diced red pepper, or fine carrot julienne for garnish

In a small bowl, dissolve the sugar in warm water and stir in the yeast. Set aside for 5 to 10 minutes.

Blend the flour with the salt and pepper.

In a large bowl, beat the eggs. Then whisk in the milk. Add the yeast and flour mixtures to the egg mixture, along with the oil, chives, and lemon zest. Blend well by hand.

In a wide pot, bring salted water to a boil. Fill a pastry bag with a ½-inch or ¾-inch round tip, with the dough. Working over the pot, carefully pipe out the dough, snipping the gnocchi off with scissors at ½-inch intervals and letting them slip into the water.

Cook the gnocchi 2 to 2½ minutes in small batches. With a slotted spoon or skimmer, transfer them to an oiled sheetpan in a single layer to cool.

In a large shallow pan, simmer the stock with the shallot, saffron, and red pepper flakes (optional) for several minutes until the saffron colors the liquid. Add the asparagus and simmer for 3 minutes. Add the gnocchi and heat through. Then toss in the crabmeat and butter. Season with salt and pepper and garnish as desired. Serve immediately.

Holly Guber

The yeast in these gnocchi makes them extra light, but if you're short on time, buy the gnocchi already prepared. Peel the asparagus to make sure that the woody stems are removed.

Breast of Duck with Gingered Apricot Sauce

Serves 4

Split the duck breasts. Trim any excess skin and score on a cross-hatch pattern. Place skin-side-down in a very hot pan. Reduce the heat to medium and season the meat with salt and pepper. Drain the fat from the pan occasionally, and cook the breasts until the skin is brown and starting to crisp. Remove from the pan and set aside.

While the breasts are cooking, place all of the sauce ingredients into a non-reactive saucepot and bring to a boil. Cover and simmer for 25 minutes, or until the apricots have softened. Pour into a blender and puree the sauce until smooth. Add the butter, season with salt and pepper, and puree again to blend.

To serve the duck, place on a rack set in a broiler pan and broil the skin side until the meat has reached the desired degree of doneness. *Be careful not to burn the skin!*

After the meat has rested, slice it thinly, and fan on the plate. Garnish with the sauce and serve.

Holly Guber

2 whole boneless duck breasts
(2 pounds)

Salt and pepper

SAUCE

4 ounces dried apricots

¼ cup white wine vinegar

¼ cup dark brown sugar,
packed

½ cup chicken stock

1 tablespoon ginger, grated

2 teaspoons shallot, chopped

2 tablespoons butter

Sweet Garlic Flan with Spring Herbs

Serves 8

2 heads garlic, split horizontally

2 tablespoons olive oil

Water or chicken stock

3 eggs

1¼ cups milk

¼ cup heavy cream

Olive oil spray

3 tablespoons fresh herbs, such as tarragon, chives, thyme, parsley, chopped

Salt

White pepper

Roast the garlic. Place the cut heads in an ovenproof pan, drizzle the cut sides with the oil, season with salt and pepper, add a little water or stock, cover with foil, and bake at 350°F. for 1 or more hours, until soft and browned. Cool slightly.

Squeeze the garlic cloves out of their skins into a bowl and whisk to smooth. Add the eggs, one at a time, then the milk, cream, and herbs. Season with salt and white pepper.

Spray 8 small (5 ounce) ramekins with olive oil and divide the custard among them evenly. Bake in a hot water bath in a 325°F. oven for 30 minutes, until custard is set. Remove from the water to cool.

To serve, reheat the flan in a 350°F. oven for 5 minutes. Unmold onto each plate.

Holly Guber

84

Semifreddo Alle Mandorle

Frozen Mousse with Amaretto, Layered with Toasted
Almonds and Crushed Amaretti

Toast the almonds in the oven, watching carefully so as not to burn. Cool completely.

Place the cooled almonds, chocolate, and cookies in a food processor and chop fine. Add the liqueur and process again to blend.

In a mixer, beat the egg whites until foamy. Add ⅓ cup sugar slowly while beating and beat until stiff, but not dry. Remove to a large mixing bowl.

In the mixer, beat the yolks with the remaining sugar and the extracts until pale yellow and thick. Add this to the whites.

Use the mixer to whip the heavy cream until stiff. Add this to the whites and yolks and fold everything together.

Use a 12-cup bowl, a 12-cup loaf pan, or 12 individual custard cups as molds. Spoon ⅓ of the nut mixture into the bottom of the mold(s). Spoon ⅓ of the egg mixture on top and tap the bottom of the mold(s) gently on a hard surface to settle the mixture in a level layer. Continue layering the nut mixture with the egg mixture in two more layers. Smooth the surface with a spatula, wrap in plastic, and freeze until hard (overnight for a single mold).

To serve, dip the mold into warm water for a few seconds before inverting onto a serving plate. Serve immediately.

Holly Guber

½ cup almonds

½ cup chopped semisweet chocolate

6 amaretto cookies or macaroons, crumbled

1 tablespoon coffee liqueur

5 eggs, separated

1 cup sugar

1 tablespoon pure almond extract

1½ teaspoons pure vanilla extract

2 cups heavy cream

SONDRA SEN has been teaching Indian cuisine at the cooking studio since its inception. She also conducts cross-cultural training for executives planning overseas business trips and is currently working on a cookbook.

Introduction to Indian Cooking

Sondra Sen

Chicken Kebab (FACING PAGE)

Coriander Chutney

Lemon Basmati Rice

Shrimp Malai Curry (ABOVE)

Green Beans with Coconut and Mustard Seeds (LEFT)

Eggplant Raita

Kheer

Chicken Kebab

Also known as chicken tikka, this preparation of marinated and broiled cubes of chicken offers an unusual combination of taste and fragrance.

3 pounds of chicken breasts, skinned, deboned, cut into one-inch pieces

2 medium-size onions, chopped

One 2-inch piece of ginger root, scraped

2 garlic cloves, chopped

4 tablespoons vegetable oil

2 tablespoons coriander powder

1 tablespoon cumin powder

½ teaspoon red pepper

2 teaspoons salt

1 cup plain yogurt

1 teaspoon roasted cumin powder (optional)

These flavor-packed chicken kebab appetizers would be welcome at any hors d'oeuvre party. Marinate the kebabs, keep them in the refrigerator, and broil them just before serving.

Heat oil in a small frying pan. When hot, add onions and sauté 4 to 5 minutes until golden brown.

Add garlic and ginger, and sauté for 1 minute.

Add coriander, cumin, red pepper, and salt. Fry for 30 seconds, stirring constantly.

Remove from heat. Set aside for 10 minutes until cool.

Add yogurt to cooled spices and blend well. Add chicken pieces. Marinate for 20 to 30 minutes.*

Spread chicken pieces on a cookie sheet and broil for 5 to 6 minutes on each side until slightly charred. Sprinkle with roasted cumin powder (optional).

Put toothpicks in each chicken tikka and serve hot as an appetizer.

VARIATION: Stuffed in pita bread or in crepes, chicken kebabs can be served as a chicken kebab sandwich, or for a luncheon menu. For this purpose, extra sauce is desirable. After frying the spices, add the chicken pieces and sauté 3 to 4 minutes on medium heat. Add yogurt and cook in an uncovered pan 5 to 6 minutes until the chicken is tender and some yogurt sauce remains.

Sondra Sen

*The chicken pieces are marinated in the cooked spices for this dish; otherwise, with the short broiling time, the spices retain a raw flavor.

Coriander Chutney

Put garlic and ginger in a blender. Switch machine on 5 to 10 seconds until finely chopped. Add onions, coriander leaves, lemon, sugar (optional), and salt (optional). Pulse several times until chutney is finely chopped.

Sondra Sen

3 cups coriander leaves, washed, coarsely chopped, tightly packed

1 garlic clove, peeled

One 2-inch piece of ginger root, scraped

¼ small onion

3 tablespoons lemon juice

1 teaspoon sugar (optional)

½ teaspoon salt (optional)

Lemon Basmati Rice

Serves 6 to 8

Place basmati rice, salt, butter, and water in a saucepan with a tight-fitting lid. Bring to a boil, reduce heat to low, and cook for approximately 20 minutes until rice is soft.

In a sauté pan, add oil and when hot, add onions and sauté until slightly brown, about 5 minutes.

Add sambar powder* and mustard seeds, and stir. Then add curry leaves, and stir 30 seconds.

Add rice and stir until spices are mixed through the rice. Then add lemon juice and mix thoroughly. Serve hot.

Sondra Sen

2 cups basmati rice

1 teaspoon salt

1 teaspoon butter

3 cups water

2 tablespoons oil

1 medium-size onion, diced

½ teaspoon sambar powder

2 teaspoons black mustard seeds

10 curry leaves

⅓ cup lemon juice

*Samber powder is a hot and spicy blend of red and black pepper, turmeric, fenugreek cumin seeds, coriander seeds, and a variety of legumes. It is a popular all-purpose spice blend used in South Indian cooking.

Shrimp Malai Curry

Serves 6 to 8

Shrimp Malai Curry is a well-known dish from Bengal in eastern India. Malai refers to a cream sauce. This recipe calls for sour cream, which thickens the sauce and enhances its flavor.

2 pounds fresh large shrimp, shelled and deveined

1 teaspoon turmeric

1 teaspoon garlic salt

4 tablespoons butter

1 cup onions, finely diced (1 large)

½ teaspoon ginger powder

¼ teaspoon ground red pepper

2 teaspoons paprika

6 cardamom seeds, pods removed, crushed

¾ cup unsweetened coconut, finely shredded or blended

1 cup sour cream

1 teaspoon salt

2 cups water

Wash the shrimp under cold water and pat dry with a paper towel.

Sprinkle the turmeric and garlic salt over the shrimp and allow to stand for one hour or overnight.

In a heavy 6-quart saucepan, heat butter and brown the onions on medium-high heat for 5 to 6 minutes until golden.

Add ginger, red pepper, and paprika and brown 1 minute.

Add shrimp and cook 2 to 3 minutes, stirring constantly until the shrimp are evenly coated with the spices.

Add cardamom seeds, coconut, sour cream, and salt. Stir until blended. Remove the shrimp.

Add water, cover the pot, and cook over medium heat for 15 minutes until the sauce thickens. Return shrimp to the pot and cook 4 to 5 minutes until tender.

Pour shrimp malai curry into a deep serving bowl and garnish with additional coconut or chopped coriander leaves.

Sondra Sen

Green Beans with Coconut and Mustard Seeds

Serves 4 to 6

Put turmeric, beans, water, and salt in a pot. Bring to a boil, cover, reduce heat, and cook about 8 to 10 minutes until tender yet still firm.

Heat oil in medium-size saucepan. Add mustard seeds. Cover and cook one minute until seeds darken and stop popping.

Add fennel seeds, coconut, and lemon juice. Cook uncovered 1 minute until most of the liquid evaporates. Cook an additional 2 to 3 minutes. Add beans and stir.

Remove from heat and garnish with coriander leaves.

Sondra Sen

¼ teaspoon turmeric

1 pound fresh green beans, cut crosswise into ½ inch thick pieces

2 cups water

1 tablespoon vegetable oil

1 teaspoon mustard seeds

1 teaspoon fennel seeds

¾ teaspoon salt

2 tablespoons unsweetened, shredded coconut

2 teaspoons lemon juice

3 tablespoons coriander leaves, chopped

Eggplant Raita

Serves 6 to 8

Brush eggplant with cooking oil. Broil in a roasting pan turning occasionally, about 20 minutes until eggplant is charred.

Cool. Remove skin. Chop eggplant.

While eggplant is roasting, heat oil in a frying pan. When hot, add chopped onions and sauté until translucent.

Add garlic and ginger and sauté 1 minute. Add cumin and stir.

Add chopped eggplant to onion and garlic mixture and store. Set aside to cool.

Add yogurt and 5 tablespoons coriander leaves. Mix and pour into serving bowl.

Garnish with remaining coriander and serve chilled.

Sondra Sen

3 medium-size eggplants

2 tablespoons vegetable oil

1 large onion, chopped fine

2 garlic cloves, crushed

1 inch piece of ginger root, scraped and finely chopped

2 teaspoons cumin powder

1 cup plain yogurt

6 tablespoons coriander leaves, chopped

Kheer

Kheer is an excellent choice for a large group and can be served elegantly in a glass punch bowl.

½ gallon milk (1%)

¾ cup sugar

½ cup uncooked, long-grained rice (basmati or texmati preferably)

½ pint heavy cream

½ cup white raisins

¼ cup slivered almonds

5 to 6 cardamom seeds, pods removed, crushed, or ¼ teaspoon rose essence or vanilla extract

Heat milk and sugar in a heavy 6-quart saucepan until it boils. Reduce heat to medium and gently boil for 10 minutes. Watch carefully so that the milk doesn't boil over or burn.

Add rice and heavy cream and stir 2 to 3 minutes. If using cardamom seeds, add at this stage.

Cook an additional 25 minutes on medium boil, stirring occasionally to avoid burning at bottom. Kheer is done when rice is soft and pudding has thickened enough to heavily coat a spoon. The kheer will further thicken after refrigeration.

Add raisins and almonds and cook another 5 minutes. Remove from heat.

When cool, add the rose or vanilla flavoring unless cardamom was added earlier.

Sondra Sen

JEAN YUEH, a native of Shanghai, is a culinary consultant who teaches and writes about Asian cuisines. One of her cookbooks won a Tastemaker Award in the Oriental category. She has traveled to Thailand and Southeast Asia to study with noted chefs and teachers.

Szechuan and Hunan Restaurant Flavors

Jean Yueh

Chicken in Spicy Sesame Sauce (ABOVE)

Shrimp in Chili Sauce (LEFT)

Hunan Beef

Mandarin Oranges in Orange Liqueur

Chicken in Spicy Sesame Sauce

1 chicken breast (1 pound) with bone and skin on (or 2 cups shredded cooked chicken meat)

4 cups fresh bean sprouts (or other vegetables)

SAUCE MIXTURE

¼ cup or more Chinese sesame seed paste

2½ tablespoons soy sauce or to taste

1 tablespoon Chinese red vinegar or to taste

½ teaspoon hot chili oil or to taste

1 teaspoon ginger, finely minced

1 teaspoon sugar

1 tablespoon sesame oil

1 tablespoon water

1 clove garlic, finely minced

1 scallion, finely minced

Boil 2 quarts of water in a saucepan. Add chicken breast, and bring the water back to a boil. Turn heat to low, and let simmer very slowly for 20 to 25 minutes.

Immediately remove the breast, and rinse it thoroughly in cold water. This can be done 1 or 2 days ahead. Before serving use your finger to shred the chicken or cut with a knife to julienne strips.

Wash and rinse bean sprouts with cold water (or, if desired, blanch them by covering with boiling water for 1 minute in a large bowl; quickly drain in a colander). Drain and dry very well before using.

In a bowl, mix sesame paste, sugar, soy sauce, sesame oil, vinegar, and water with a spoon until the mixture becomes a smooth paste. More water can be added if the sauce is too thick. If the sauce is too thin, add more sesame paste. Add finely minced ginger and garlic and hot chili oil to taste.

After draining sprouts, place in a salad bowl or serving dish, then top with chicken strips. Pour the sauce over, toss to mix. Sprinkle finely minced scallions on top and serve.

Jean Yueh

Shrimp in Chili Sauce

Serves 2 to 4

Shell and devein the shrimp. Wash and drain in a colander. Pat very dry with paper towels.

Mince ginger and garlic. Chop scallions.

Mix the sauce ingredients except cornstarch in a bowl. Mix cornstarch with water in a small bowl.

Heat the wok over high heat until very hot. Add 2 tablespoons oil and heat the oil until it is very hot. Add shrimp, stirring until just cooked, about 2 minutes. Remove from the wok.

Heat 1 tablespoon oil in the wok over medium heat. Fry crushed red pepper, ginger, and garlic for about 30 seconds; do not burn garlic. Add scallion, snow peas, and water chestnuts, and cook for about 30 seconds. Add the sauce ingredients and bring to a boil. Return the shrimp. Give the cornstarch mixture a good stir and add to the sauce, stirring until the sauce is thickened and turns translucent. Add sesame oil (optional) and serve.

Jean Yueh

The trick to stir-frying is to keep the wok very hot and the food moving. Do not overload the pan. If you have too much food in the pan at once, you'll steam it in its own liquid rather than stir-fry.

1 pound shrimp with shell (25 to 30 count in a pound)

4 ounces fresh snow peas, wash and string

4 ounces sliced water chestnuts

1 tablespoon ginger, minced

1 tablespoon garlic, minced

2 scallions, chopped

1 teaspoon crushed red pepper or to taste

3 tablespoons cooking oil

1 tablespoon sesame oil (optional)

SAUCE

6 tablespoons ketchup

3 tablespoons soy sauce

2 tablespoons dry sherry

3 tablespoons sugar

¼ teaspoon salt or to taste

¾ cup water

4 teaspoons cornstarch in 3 tablespoons water

Hunan Beef

¾ pound flank steak or tender beef

MARINADE

2 tablespoons soy sauce or to taste

1 tablespoon dry sherry

1 teaspoon cornstarch

SAUCE MIXTURE

2 tablespoons soy sauce or to taste

1½ teaspoons wine vinegar

1 tablespoon dry sherry

½ teaspoon sugar

2 teaspoons cornstarch

¼ cup water

2 large leeks, about 1 pound (white and light green parts only)

1 tablespoon ginger, finely minced

1 tablespoon garlic, finely minced

1 teaspoon crushed red pepper or to taste

3 tablespoons cooking oil

Partially frozen meat is easier to slice. Cut beef across the grain into bite-size pieces, about ⅛ inch thick. Mix with the marinade. Mix the sauce ingredients in a bowl.

Cut leeks into 1½-inch slanted sections, then cut the section lengthwise into halves. Separate them into individual petals. Wash leeks in a large bowl filled with water, stirring to let the sandy particles settle down to the bottom of the bowl. Remove the leeks, and repeat this washing process a few times until there are no more sandy particles. Drain in a colander. Mince ginger and garlic.

Heat the wok until very hot, add 3 tablespoons oil, and heat until hot. Add ginger, garlic, and crushed red pepper. Cook for few seconds but don't let them burn. Quickly add the beef, stirring until beef is just cooked, about 1 to 2 minutes. Remove from the wok.

Add 1 tablespoon oil, if necessary, to the wok. Over medium heat stir-fry the leeks for about 1 minute. Return the beef. Give the sauce mixture a good stir and add to the wok. Stir over high heat until it thickens and coats the meat. Remove from the wok and serve.

Jean Yueh

Mandarin Oranges in Orange Liqueur

Serves 4

This is a refreshing and quick recipe, and is wonderful to serve at the end of a Chinese meal.

Mix orange liqueur with mandarin oranges and their juice in a pretty serving bowl. Place in the refrigerator for 1 hour or until it is chilled. Serve in individual dessert cups.

For an added touch, peel one large orange as thinly as possible with a potato peeler, leaving the white pith on the orange. Cut peel into very thin julienne strips.

In a small saucepan, heat 3 tablespoons sugar, 3 tablespoons water, orange peel, and a pinch of cream of tartar to a boil. Simmer for 10 minutes or until thick and syrupy. Cool to room temperature.

Just before serving, spoon orange peel and syrup over mandarin oranges.

Jean Yueh

One 16-ounce can mandarin oranges

3 tablespoons orange liqueur or to taste

1 large orange (optional)

3 tablespoons water (optional)

3 tablespoons sugar (optional)

Pinch cream of tartar (optional)

KATHLEEN K. SANDERSON, a graduate of the California Culinary Institute, is Consulting Food Editor of *Restaurant Business* magazine. In addition, Kathleen serves as a consultant to several food companies.

Make Ahead Buffet

Kathleen K. Sanderson

Artichoke and Herb Pizzas (ABOVE)

Lemon Ginger Muffins with Smoked Ham

Roasted Filet of Beef with Cabernet Butter Sauce

Tomatoes Persillé (LEFT)

Creamy Carrot Puree

Triple Chocolate Brownies (FACING PAGE)

Artichoke and Herb Pizzas

Serves 8 to 10

One 8-ounce package low fat cream cheese

1 cup grated mozzarella

1 cup freshly grated Parmesan cheese, divided

One 14-ounce can artichokes, drained, rinsed, and chopped

½ cup diced roasted red pepper

¼ cup parsley, chopped

¼ cup chives, chopped

Salt and pepper to taste

5 pocketless pitas

Preheat oven to 400°F.

In a bowl, mix together cream cheese, mozzarella, and half of the Parmesan until well blended. Add artichokes, red pepper, and herbs.

Season mixture to taste (this mixture can be made up to 5 days in advance).

Place pitas on a clean work surface. Divide cheese mixture among the 5 rounds and spread evenly leaving a ½-inch border all around, sprinkle with remaining cheese.

Bake pizzas 2 or 3 at a time for 10 to 12 minutes or until golden brown.

Let pizzas cool slightly before cutting into 6 wedges. Serve hot.

Kathleen K. Sanderson

Lemon Ginger Muffins with Smoked Ham

Makes 28 Small Muffins or 12 Large Muffins

Lightly grease 2 mini-muffin pans or 1 muffin tin (12).

Preheat oven to 350°F.

Sift together flour, soda, ground ginger, and salt. Set aside.

With a mixer, cream together the sugar and butter. Add the eggs and mix well. Add the flour and buttermilk alternately ending with flour. (This is a basic muffin batter.)

Fold in walnuts, raisins, fresh ginger, and lemon zest. Scoop into prepared muffin tins and bake mini muffins for 18 to 20 minutes and large muffins for 22 to 25 minutes. Cool on a rack and serve with butter or as directed below.

2 cups flour

1 teaspoon baking soda

1 teaspoon ground ginger

½ teaspoon salt

1 stick sweet butter

1 cup sugar

2 eggs

1 cup buttermilk

1 cup toasted walnuts, chopped

1 cup golden raisins or dried cranberries

2 tablespoons fresh ginger (2 inches), chopped

1 tablespoon lemon zest

Smoked Ham and Honey Mustard Filled Muffins

Split cooled mini-muffins.

Spread honey mustard on bottom and top with ½ slice smoked ham that has been folded to fit.

Place muffin top back on and serve as appetizer.

Kathleen K. Sanderson

½ pound sliced smoked ham

⅓ cup honey mustard

Roasted Filet of Beef with Cabernet Butter Sauce

Serves 10

1 whole filet, trimmed and tied (3½ to 4 pounds trimmed weight)

Salt and pepper

2 tablespoons oil

½ cup cabernet wine

2½ cups cabernet sauce

Preheat oven to 400°F.

Rub filet with oil and liberally season with salt and pepper. Heat a large skillet and sear filet on all sides until golden. (You can use an outdoor grill to do this step.) Transfer filet to a roasting pan. (This can be done in the morning. Refrigerate meat until 1 hour before it is ready to go into the oven.)

Add wine to the skillet. Turn heat up to medium and simmer, scraping up all the bits. Cook briefly until the liquid is slightly syrupy. Strain and set aside. Place filet in preheated oven and let roast 30 to 35 minutes (8 minutes per pound of meat after searing). Take the meat out when meat thermometer registers 130°F. Let the meat rest 10 to 15 minutes loosely tented with foil. Slice filet and serve with Cabernet Butter Sauce.

Cabernet Butter Sauce

1 quart quality beef stock, heated

3 tablespoons unsalted butter

⅓ cup flour

1 carrot, celery stalk, and small onion, minced

1 cup Madeira wine

½ cup shallot (2 to 3), minced

1½ cups cabernet wine

¼ cup unsalted butter

2 to 3 tablespoons parsley, chopped

Salt and pepper to taste

In a heavy gauge 3-quart sauce pan, melt the butter, whisk in the flour, and cook on low heat for 15 to 20 minutes until nut brown (this is a roux). Stir occasionally to avoid burning. Add minced vegetables and continue to cook 3 to 4 minutes.

Slowly add heated stock to the roux mixture. Bring the sauce to a boil. Add Madeira and reduce heat to a simmer. Simmer sauce until it reduces by half (about 45 minutes). Strain sauce and set aside. (This is a demi-glace.)

In a saucepan combine shallot and wine. Bring to a simmer and reduce to a syrupy glaze. Add strained demi-glace and bring to a boil. Season sauce, remove from heat, add reserved strained cabernet (from filet), and swirl in butter and parsley. Serve sauce as directed.

Kathleen K. Sanderson

Tomatoes Persillé

Preheat oven to 400°F.

Core tomatoes and slice in half. Slice a small piece off of the tomatoes on the rounded side so they lie flat on a plate.

Place tomatoes in an oven-to-table dish. Drizzle with olive oil and sprinkle with salt and pepper. In a bowl, combine bread crumbs, parsley, and Parmesan. Top each tomato with the mixture. Roast tomatoes for 15 to 18 minutes in preheated oven and serve with roasted meats.

NOTE: Crumb mixture can be used as a stuffing, coating for lamb, or topping for various casseroles. Mixture can be made several days in advance.

Kathleen K. Sanderson

5 plum tomatoes

2 tablespoons olive oil

½ cup fresh bread crumbs (¼ cup dried)

¼ cup parsley, chopped

¼ cup Parmesan cheese, grated

Cracked pepper

Salt

Creamy Carrot Puree

Serves 8 to 10

Two 1-pound bags peeled baby carrots

4 tablespoons butter

½ cup cream (more if necessary)

Salt, white pepper, and nutmeg

Chopped parsley

Butter a 1-quart shallow casserole dish.

In a 3-quart sauce pan, combine carrots and enough water to cover carrots. Bring to a boil, reduce heat, and simmer carrots for 12 to 14 minutes or until very tender. Drain carrots and transfer to a food processor. Puree carrots with butter until smooth.

While motor is running add enough cream to create a creamy puree. Season puree and transfer to prepared casserole. The carrots can be prepared up to two days before this point.

Heat carrots in a 375°F. to 400°F. oven for 12 to 15 minutes. Sprinkle with parsley and serve.

Kathleen K. Sanderson

Triple Chocolate Brownies

Serves 10 to 12

6 ounces good quality bitter or dark sweet chocolate

2 ounces unsweetened chocolate

¾ cup sweet butter (1½ sticks)

1½ cups sugar

4 large eggs

1 teaspoon vanilla

1 cup flour

½ teaspoon salt

1 cup semisweet chocolate chips

1 cup chopped toasted pecans or walnuts

If you don't have bittersweet or dark chocolate, you can substitute an equal amount of semisweet.

Preheat oven to 350°F.

In a double boiler or microwave, melt dark and unsweetened chocolate and butter. Stir to create a smooth mixture and cool slightly. (Microwave at full power for 1 minute and then in 30 second intervals, stirring between each interval.)

Combine sugar, eggs, and vanilla, and mix well. Add chocolate mixture and mix well. Add flour and salt, and mix to just combine. Stir in chocolate chips and nuts.

Pour batter into a greased 9 × 13 × 2-inch pan lined with buttered parchment and bake for 30 to 35 minutes or until knife comes clean.

Cool brownies 15 minutes in pan before turning onto a board to cut. Cool brownies completely before cutting into squares or triangles.

NOTE: Brownies can be cut and frozen several weeks in advance. They can be made 3 to 4 days in advance and kept in an airtight container at room temperature.

Kathleen K. Sanderson

MARLA MENDELSOHN, Certified Culinary Profesional, is owner of
Cook Ease catering and event planning. She teaches culinary arts in the New
Jersey–New York area with a focus on multigenerational programs, and also
serves as a product development consultant to food companies. Marla
studied at the Ritz Escoffier, Paris, and is a member of the IACP and NYACP.
She is the creator of a children's cooking video, *Kids Can Cook*.

Rosh Hashanah Dinner

Marla Mendelsohn

Triple Mustard and Honey
Chicken (LEFT)

Potato Pancake Wedge

Mixed Greens with Apple
Dressing (ABOVE)

Spiced and Stacked
Apple Cake

Triple Mustard and Honey Chicken

Serves 6

3 pounds boneless chicken breasts

Salt

Freshly ground pepper

1/3 cup olive oil

2 tablespoons olive oil

1 teaspoon Tabasco sauce (divided use)

2 tablespoons Dijon mustard

2 tablespoons honey mustard

1 teaspoon dry mustard

3 tablespoons honey

1 teaspoon salt

1/2 teaspoon freshly ground pepper

1 tablespoon minced shallot

2 teaspoons white wine vinegar

3/4 cup flour

1/2 cup honey crunch wheat germ

Season the chicken liberally with salt and pepper. Marinate the chicken in 1/3 cup olive oil and 3/4 teaspoon Tabasco sauce for 30 to 60 minutes.

Mix the 3 mustards, honey, salt, and pepper. Stir in the shallot. Blend in the vinegar, 2 tablespoons olive oil, and 1/4 teaspoon Tabasco sauce.

Preheat the oven to 350°F. Mix flour with wheat germ.

Remove the chicken from the marinade. Discard the marinade.

Paint the chicken pieces with the mustard/honey mixture. Dredge the chicken in flour–wheat germ mixture. Place the chicken pieces on a foil-lined roasting pan and bake for about 20 minutes. Serve.

Marla Mendelsohn

Potato Pancake Wedge

Serves 8

1 pound onions

10 ounces zucchini, trimmed

3 1/4 pounds russet potatoes, peeled

2 teaspoons salt

4 tablespoons vegetable oil

4 tablespoons margarine

Preheat oven to 450°F.

Coarsely grate onions, zucchini, and then potatoes with medium shredding disc of food processor. Divide mixture into two batches and wrap in two kitchen towels. Squeeze out as much liquid as possible. Place mixture in large bowl, add salt, and blend.

Heat 2 tablespoons of oil and 2 tablespoons of margarine in 2 large nonstick ovenproof skillets over medium high heat. Add half of the potato mixture to each skillet. Press mixture firmly to even thickness. Cook 4 minutes. Reduce heat to medium and cook until bottom is golden brown, sliding spatula under pancakes occasionally to prevent sticking, about 6 more minutes.

Place skillet in oven. Bake until tops are firm, about 14 minutes. Use broiler for 2 minutes to brown top, if necessary.

NOTE: Can be made ahead and rewarmed in 400°F. oven until crisp.

Marla Mendelsohn

When you're having company, these large potato pancakes are much easier than lots of small ones. Use a starchy potato such as a russet—it will hold together better. Make the pancakes ahead and reheat them on a cookie sheet when you're ready.

Mixed Greens with Apple Dressing

Serves 4

Whisk vinegar and oil in a large bowl. Season with salt and pepper.

Stir in apple. Let apple marinate at room temperature for 30 minutes.

Add greens to dressing and toss to coat.

Marla Mendelsohn

3 tablespoons apple cider vinegar

3 tablespoons walnut oil

1 large red apple, cored and cut into ½-inch cubes

8 cups mixed salad greens (about 5 ounces)

Spiced and Stacked Apple Cake

FILLING

3¼ cups water

½ cup brown sugar

¼ cup apple juice

1 teaspoon vanilla

Two 6-ounce packages dried apples

CAKE

½ cup vegetable shortening

1 cup brown sugar

⅓ cup molasses

1 teaspoon vanilla

3 eggs

2¼ cups flour

1¼ teaspoons baking soda

½ teaspoon nutmeg

½ teaspoon cinnamon

½ teaspoon allspice

¼ teaspoon salt

¾ cup low-fat buttermilk

Cooking spray

2 tablespoons confectioners' sugar

Combine all filling ingredients in a large saucepan and bring to a boil. Cover, reduce heat, and simmer for 35 minutes, until liquid is nearly absorbed. Puree apple mixture in a food processor, using 8 to 9 pulses, until a chunky mixture is formed.

Preheat oven to 350°F.

To make the cake, beat shortening with brown sugar until light and fluffy. Add molasses, vanilla, and eggs, and beat well.

Mix flour with baking soda, nutmeg, cinnamon, allspice, and salt. Add flour mixture to sugar mixture alternately with buttermilk, beginning and ending with flour mixture.

Pour batter into a 12-cup Bundt pan sprayed with cooking spray. Bake for 40 minutes. (A toothpick inserted should come out clean.) Cool 10 minutes and then remove from pan and cool on wire rack.

Cut cake in thirds horizontally using a serrated knife. Place bottom layer on serving plate cut side up. Spread with half of apple filling. Place middle layer on top and spread with remaining half of filling. Place top layer on and sprinkle with confectioners' sugar.

Marla Mendelsohn

JEAN YUEH, a native of Shanghai, is a culinary consultant who teaches and writes about Asian cuisines. One of her cookbooks won a Tastemaker Award in the Oriental category. She has traveled to Thailand and Southeast Asia to study with noted chefs and teachers.

International Tofu Flavors

Jean Yueh

Cream of Broccoli Soup (LEFT)

Teriyaki Tofu and Vegetables (ABOVE)

Pumpkin Mousse

Cream of Broccoli Soup

Serves 6

One 12.3 ounce pack lite firm silken tofu, cut into eight pieces

10 ounces broccoli (approximately 1 small head)

½ cup onions, peeled and sliced (approximately 1 small)

2 cloves garlic, peeled and chopped

4 ounces Idaho potato (approximately 1 medium potato)

1 tablespoon olive oil or cooking oil

3 cups chicken broth or vegetable broth or to desired thickness

½ teaspoon ground nutmeg

¼ teaspoon ground cumin or to taste

½ teaspoon salt or to taste

¼ teaspoon ground pepper

Dash cayenne pepper (optional)

1 teaspoon lemon juice (optional)

Cut off tough ends of broccoli, then cut them into bite-size pieces. Peel potato and cut into ½-inch cubes.

In a large pot, heat oil over medium heat. Sauté onion and garlic until onion is translucent, being careful not to burn them. Add broth and bring to a boil. Add broccoli and potato and bring back to boiling. Reduce heat and let it simmer for about 8 minutes or until potato is tender.

Puree the soup and tofu in the blender in batches. When very smooth, return the puree into the pot. Add nutmeg, cumin, salt, pepper, cayenne pepper (optional), and lemon juice (optional) to taste and reheat the soup before serving. If the soup becomes too thick, add more broth to the desired thickness.

Jean Yueh

Teriyaki Tofu and Vegetables

Serves 3 to 4

Heat the sauce ingredients in a small saucepan, until sugar is dissolved. Let cool to room temperature.

Toast sesame seeds (if used) in a frying pan over medium heat until golden yellow.

Marinate the tofu and vegetables in the teriyaki sauce for half an hour. Do not overmarinate the tofu, as it may get too salty.

Spray a skillet with cooking spray (or use a non-stick skillet). Heat until hot. Cook the tofu and vegetable in one layer until the tofu is heated through, and the vegetable to the desired doneness. Place on a serving platter. Sprinkle with sesame seeds and serve with extra sauce.

Jean Yueh

1 pound extra-firm or firm tofu, cut into 2 × 1¾ × ¾-inch pieces

1 red bell pepper, cut into 1-inch pieces

6 cremini or button mushrooms, cut into halves

1 medium onion, sliced; break into petals

2 tablespoons sesame seeds

Cooking spray

TERIYAKI SAUCE

½ cup soy sauce or to taste

¼ cup sake or dry sherry

2 tablespoons sugar

1½ tablespoons ginger, minced

¼ cup water

Pumpkin Mousse

1 cup canned pumpkin puree
(unsweetened)

18 ounces (1½ packages of a
12-ounce) low fat, firm silken
tofu

1 envelope unflavored gelatine

¼ cup sugar or to taste

¼ cup dark brown sugar

¼ teaspoon salt

¼ teaspoon cinnamon

¼ teaspoon cloves

¼ teaspoon nutmeg

Cooking spray

6 tablespoons candied ginger
(optional)

¾ cup maple syrup (optional)

Whipped cream (optional)

Add ¼ cup cold water to a small bowl. Sprinkle the gelatine over the water
and let it stand for 2 minutes.

In a saucepan, heat the pumpkin, sugar, and salt together over medium heat
until the sugar is dissolved. Add gelatine, cinnamon, cloves, and nutmeg,
stirring until the gelatine is dissolved. Crumble up the tofu and mix with the
pumpkin mixture.

Place the mixture in a blender and process until the mixture is thoroughly
blended. Spray 6 small Pyrex bowls generously with cooking spray. Pour the
pumpkin mixture into the bowls. Refrigerate for 3 hours or longer or until
they are set. Invert each onto a dessert plate. Serve as is or with optional
topping.

Optional Topping: Mince 6 tablespoons candied ginger, then add to ¾ cup
maple syrup in a small saucepan. Heat until just beginning to boil. Remove
from the heat. Pour on top of the pumpkin mousse. For more flavor, top the
sauce with whipped cream.

Jean Yueh

WINTER

STEPHEN SCHMIDT is a cooking teacher, food historian, and a regular contributor to *Cook's Illustrated* magazine. He is the author of *Master Recipes* and is currently working on *Dessert in America*, a baking book and history of American dessert. Schmidt was also a major contributor to the new edition of *The Joy of Cooking*.

A Holiday Roast Beef Dinner

Stephen Schmidt

Parsnip Soup with Apples and Fresh Thyme (LEFT)

Beef Strip Loin Roast with Spicy Mushroom Gravy (OPPOSITE PAGE)

Mashed Potatoes with Roasted Garlic

Green Beans with Roasted Red Peppers and Balsamic Vinaigrette (ABOVE)

Boston Cream Pie Trifle

Parsnip Soup with Apples and Fresh Thyme

SOUP

1½ pounds parsnips

6 cups water

4 teaspoons fresh thyme leaves

2 teaspoons sugar

2 teaspoons salt

8 tablespoons (1 stick) unsalted butter

3 cups onions, finely chopped

2 cups celery, finely chopped

2 pounds (4 large) Granny Smith apples

Additional water as needed

1 cup light cream (or ½ cup each heavy cream and milk)

3 to 4 tablespoons strained fresh lemon juice

4 to 5 tablespoons cognac

Freshly ground white pepper

GARNISH

½ pound parsnips

4 tablespoons unsalted butter

1½ teaspoons very carefully picked fresh thyme leaves

Peel the parsnips and cut crosswise into ½-inch slices. Put the parsnips in a saucepan, cover with water, and add thyme leaves, sugar, and salt. Bring to a simmer and cook, covered, for about 30 minutes, or until the parsnips give no resistance when pierced with a knife.

In the meantime, melt the butter over moderate heat in a large, heavy saucepan or pot. Add onions and celery and cook slowly for about 10 minutes, or until vegetables are soft, but not brown. Peel apples and shred down to the core on the shredding plate of a box grater. Add apples to onions and celery and cook slowly, covered, for about 20 minutes, or until the apples are very tender. Be careful not to let the mixture brown.

Combine the parsnips, including their cooking liquid, and apples, then puree very thoroughly in a blender or with a hand blender. (If you are using a blender, you will need to puree the soup in four batches.) Return the soup to the pot and add enough water to thin to soup consistency. Cover the pan and let the soup stand over the lowest possible flame for at least 15 minutes to blend the flavors. Stir in the cream (or milk and cream) and season the soup with lemon juice, cognac, and white pepper.

To make the garnish, peel the parsnips and cut in matchsticks 1½ inches long and ⅛-inch wide. Heat the butter to sizzling in a large skillet, add the parsnips, and cook over moderately high heat, stirring often, until the parsnips are a rich nut brown. Using a slotted spoon, remove the parsnips to paper towels and let drain. Ladle a cup (or a little less) of soup into each bowl and sprinkle with the fried parsnips and a pinch of fresh thyme leaves.

NOTE: The base of the soup may be prepared 3 days ahead; cover and refrigerate. Add cream, seasonings, and garnish just before serving.

Stephen Schmidt

Beef Strip Loin Roast with Spicy Mushroom Gravy

Serves 10

For the gravy, combine the ground beef, beef broth, wine, onion, garlic, thyme, cloves, and bay leaf in a wide saucepan and simmer very slowly for 45 minutes. Strain the broth into a small saucepan, pressing down firmly on the solids before discarding. You should have at least 3¼ cups of broth; if you have less, add water.

Rinse out and lightly dry (with paper towels) the saucepan you used to prepare the broth. Place the butter in the pan and heat over a moderately high flame until it just begins to color.

Add the mushrooms and, tossing constantly with a wooden spoon, sauté until wilted and cooked through. Stirring constantly, sprinkle the flour over the mushrooms (the mixture will look very dry) and cook, still stirring, until the flour clinging to the saucepan begins to toast. Remove the pan from heat.

Bring the strained stock to a boil and pour it all at once over the mushrooms, stirring constantly. Set the saucepan over moderate heat, bring the sauce to a simmer, and, scraping the pan with the wooden spoon to dissolve all the flour, cook the sauce until thickened. Add the brandy, pepper, and mustard and simmer slowly until the sauce is thick and flavorful, 10 to 20 minutes. Season with salt, if needed. Slide the sauce off the heat and cover until needed.

GRAVY

1 pound extra-lean ground beef

3½ cups (two 13½-ounce cans) beef broth

2 cups dry, full-bodied red wine

1 cup onions, chopped

3 tablespoons garlic, finely chopped

1 teaspoon whole dried thyme

6 whole cloves

2 bay leaves

4 tablespoons (½ stick) unsalted butter

6 ounces portobella mushrooms (weighed without stems), thinly sliced

6 ounces shiitake mushrooms, stems removed and thinly sliced

¼ cup all-purpose flour (measure by dip-and-sweep)

2 tablespoons brandy or cognac

1 teaspoon freshly ground black pepper, or more to taste

1 teaspoon dry mustard

ROAST

One beef strip loin roast weighing about 5 pounds

Salt

Freshly ground black pepper

Set a rack in the lower-middle level of the oven and heat the oven to 425°F.

Dry the roast with paper towels, season highly with salt and pepper, and arrange fat side up on a rack set in a roasting pan. For rare/medium-rare, roast until a meat thermometer inserted in the thickest part registers 110°F. to 115°F., 40 to 55 minutes; for medium-rare/medium, roast to 120°F. to 130°F., 50 to 65 minutes. Let the roast stand 15 minutes; the temperature will rise 10°F. to 15°F. Slice thin and serve with the gravy.

NOTE: The gravy can refrigerated, covered, for 4 days.

Stephen Schmidt

Mashed Potatoes with Roasted Garlic

Serves 10

5 large heads garlic

Olive oil

5 pounds baking potatoes

1½ cups milk

¾ cup (1½ sticks) unsalted butter

2 teaspoons salt

1 to 2 teaspoons freshly ground white pepper, to taste

Remove excess layers of papery skin from garlic, then cut about ¼ inch off the tops of the heads. A few cloves around the outside of the heads will remain whole; cut off tips of these individually.

Film the cut portion of the garlic with oil, then wrap each head in foil, shiny side in. Bake at 350°F. for about 45 minutes, or until the outside cloves are brownish and translucent and the whole head is very soft. Unwrap the garlic and let cool, then squeeze out the pulp and mash lightly with a fork.

Peel potatoes and cut crosswise in 1½-inch chunks. Simmer, covered, in well-salted water for about 20 minutes, or until completely tender. Drain, reserving a little of the cooking water, put through a ricer or food mill, and return to the pot.

Combine the milk, butter, and mashed garlic in a saucepan and heat until the mixture is steaming hot. Slowly whisk mixture into the riced potatoes. Season with salt and pepper. Keep warm over low heat for a few minutes before serving to allow flavors to blend.

NOTE: For best flavor and texture, make the potatoes no more than 2 hours ahead. To keep warm, spoon the potatoes into a bowl and place the bottom of the bowl in a pot of water maintained at just below the simmer. Stir occasionally; do *not* cover. Alternatively, prepare the potatoes up to 3 days ahead; let cool, then cover and refrigerate. To serve, spoon the potatoes into a buttered baking dish and let stand several hours at room temperature, then place in a 300°F. oven, uncovered, until warmed through, 20 to 30 minutes.

Stephen Schmidt

Green Beans with Roasted Red Peppers and Balsamic Vinaigrette

Serves 10

Cut the tops and bottoms off the peppers, cut a slit down the pepper bodies, and open the peppers out flat. Remove the seeds and cut away the whitish ribs. Lay the pepper bodies, tops, and bottoms skin-side-up on a baking sheet and broil until the skins blister and char. Place peppers in a paper bag and let stand 10 minutes. Slip off skins. Cut the peppers into strips just a little more than 1/8 inch wide.

For the vinaigrette, whisk together the olive oil, mustard, anchovy paste, salt, pepper, and oregano, then slowly beat in the balsamic vinegar.

Boil the beans in a large quantity of well-salted water until done to taste. Drain thoroughly and toss with the pepper strips and vinaigrette.

NOTE: The peppers can be made several days ahead and stored in the refrigerator in a covered container. The vinaigrette can be made any time on the day of serving.

Stephen Schmidt

3 large-medium red bell peppers

2½ pounds green beans

⅓ cup extra-virgin olive oil

1 tablespoon Dijon mustard

¾ teaspoon anchovy paste

¾ teaspoon salt

¾ teaspoon freshly ground black pepper

Heaping ¼ teaspoon dried oregano, crumbled

3 tablespoons balsamic vinegar

Boston Cream Pie Trifle

CUSTARD

12 large egg yolks

1 cup sugar

2 teaspoons pure vanilla extract

¼ teaspoon salt

4 cups whole milk

RUM-SOAKED LADY FINGERS

½ cup boiling water

¼ cup sugar

⅓ cup dark Jamaican rum

2 dozen 4-inch dry lady fingers (also called Savoidardi or champagne biscuits)

CHOCOLATE GLAZE

8 ounces semisweet or bittersweet chocolate, chopped in ¼- to ½-inch pieces

1 cup heavy cream

4 tablespoons (½ stick) unsalted butter

¼ cup light corn syrup

WHIPPED CREAM AND GARNISH

3 cups heavy cream

¾ cup confectioners' sugar

1 teaspoon pure vanilla extract

1½ ounces semisweet or bittersweet chocolate

Make the custard. Set a rack in the lower-middle level of the oven and heat the oven to 300°F. Cover the bottom of a roasting pan with three layers of paper towels and place a 9 × 13 × 2-inch glass baking dish inside the roasting pan. Have 2 quarts of simmering water ready.

Combine the egg yolks, sugar, vanilla, and salt in a mixing bowl and whisk just until blended. Stirring constantly, warm the milk in a medium saucepan over moderate heat until it begins to steam. Whisking gently, slowly pour the hot milk into the egg mixture, then whisk a moment longer to dissolve the sugar.

Strain the custard into the glass baking dish, then skim the foam off the top with a spoon. Pour simmering water into the roasting pan to the depth of the custard. Loosely drape a sheet of aluminum foil over the custard (*not* over the entire roasting pan). Bake the custard until softly set, something like yogurt, 1 hour or a little longer. Let the custard stand at room temperature until lukewarm, then remove from the water bath and refrigerate, still covered with foil, until cold.

Moisten the lady fingers. Combine the boiling water and sugar in a small mixing bowl and stir until the sugar is dissolved. Stir in the rum. Lay out the lady fingers on a large baking sheet and brush both sides with the syrup, using it all. Push the lady fingers together into 2 slabs of 12 lady fingers each. Cover the lady fingers with plastic wrap and let stand at least 30 minutes to soften.

Make the chocolate glaze. Place the chopped chocolate in a mixing bowl. Stirring constantly, heat the cream, butter, and corn syrup in a medium saucepan over moderate heat until the mixture comes to a boil. Immediately pour the cream mixture over the chocolate. Let stand 2 minutes, then whisk smooth. Refrigerate, stirring occasionally, until the consistency of sour cream; that is, just thick enough to spread, 30 minutes to 1 hour. Spread the mixture over the two slabs of lady fingers, then refrigerate until the glaze is firm and set.

Assemble the trifle. Cut the lady fingers apart with a metal spatula or bench scraper. Cover the bottom of a 3- to 4-quart footed glass trifle dish or deep glass bowl with half the lady fingers, arranging the lady fingers on their sides and pressing an unbroken ring of lady fingers, chocolate side facing out, around the inside of the dish. Spoon the custard over the top. Cover the custard with the remaining lady fingers, arranged as before. Cover the dish with plastic wrap and refrigerate for at least 1 hour, preferably for 12 hours, or for up to 2 days if more convenient.

Make the topping no more than 12 hours before you plan to serve the trifle. Beat the cream at moderately high speed with an electric mixer until it begins to thicken. Add the confectioners' sugar and vanilla and continue to beat the cream until stiff. Spoon the cream over the top of the trifle or, for a more decorative effect, pipe the cream through a large star tip.

For the decoration, melt 1½ ounces chocolate and spread in a 6 × 10-inch rectangle on a sheet of waxed paper. Slip the chocolate onto a baking sheet and freeze until firm—just a few minutes—then peel off the paper and cut the chocolate into thin strips or other shapes of your choosing and press onto the whipped cream.

Stephen Schmidt

MARLA MENDELSOHN, Certified Culinary Professional, is owner of Cook Ease catering and event planning. She teaches culinary arts in the New Jersey–New York area with a focus on multigenerational programs, and also serves as a product development consultant to food companies. Marla studied at the Ritz Escoffier, Paris, and is a member of the IACP and NYACP. She is the creator of a children's cooking video, *Kids Can Cook*.

Chanukah Dinner

Marla Mendelsohn

Potato Pancakes (Latkes) Filled with Wild Mushrooms (LEFT)

Roasted Root Vegetables (ABOVE)

Stuffed Veal with Lemon Parsley Sauce (OPPOSITE PAGE)

Carrot Soup

Chocolate Soufflé

Potato Pancakes (Latkes) Filled with Wild Mushrooms

Serves 4

¾ pound wild mushrooms (porcini, crimini, chanterelles, morels, or oyster)

¼ cup butter or margarine

4 cloves garlic, minced

2 tablespoons parsley, chopped

1½ pounds russet potatoes, grated and peeled

1 onion, grated

1 teaspoon salt

2 eggs

½ teaspoon pepper

¼ cup flour

½ cup bread crumbs

Vegetable oil for frying

Cut mushrooms into small pieces. Heat butter or margarine in sauté pan. Sauté mushrooms and garlic until liquid given off by mushrooms evaporates, about 10 minutes. Add parsley. Set aside.

Mix potatoes with onion, salt, pepper, eggs, flour, and bread crumbs.

Heat oil in large sauté pan. Form latkes with ½ cup latke mixture and press with a spatula to compress.

Top latkes with a tablespoon of mushrooms. Cover mushrooms with more latke mixture and flip, cooking on both sides. Serve hot.

Marla Mendelsohn

Roasted Root Vegetables

Serves 4

Preheat oven to 400°F.

Put whole, unpeeled head of garlic in saucepan and cover with water. Bring to a boil and then simmer to soften cloves and loosen skins, about 10 minutes. Drain and refresh garlic head under cold water. Separate cloves and peel.

Put vegetables, excluding garlic, into a roasting pan. Do not overcrowd. Toss vegetables with oil and sprinkle with salt. Roast, stirring or shaking every 15 minutes, until evenly browned and tender, about 45 minutes. Add peeled garlic during the last 15 minutes of roasting. Sprinkle with pepper. Serve hot or at room temperature.

Marla Mendelsohn

1 head garlic

2 pounds root vegetable, peeled and cut into 1-inch pieces: carrots, turnips, parsnips, onions, potatoes, sweet potatoes

1 medium onion or 4 to 6 shallots, peeled

2 tablespoons vegetable oil

Salt

Pepper

Stuffed Veal with Lemon Parsley Sauce

Serves 4

Two 10-ounce boxes frozen chopped spinach

3 tablespoons margarine or butter

2 tablespoons vegetable oil

1 small onion, chopped fine

Salt

Freshly ground pepper

1 pound veal, single slice, cut or pounded to ³⁄₈ inch thick (shoulder, rump, or top round)

¹⁄₂ cup dry white wine

Defrost spinach and squeeze dry.

Sauté chopped onion in 1 tablespoon margarine or butter and 1 tablespoon oil until golden brown. Add chopped spinach, salt, and freshly ground pepper. Cook for 1 minute, stirring constantly.

Lay the veal flat on a work surface. Spread spinach and onion mixture over veal, distributing it evenly. Roll veal, jelly-roll style, so that the grain in the veal is parallel to the length of the roll. Secure the roll with kitchen string.

Heat the remaining margarine or butter and oil in a medium sauce pot. Add the rolled veal and brown on all sides over medium high heat. Add salt and pepper and the wine. Lower the heat and cook with a cover slightly askew for about 1¹⁄₂ hours. Turn veal every 20 minutes. There should be no liquid left in the pot except for some concentrated cooking juices. Do not wash the pot. Transfer veal to serving platter and pour sauce over top.

Marla Mendelsohn

Lemon Parsley Sauce

1 large bunch Italian parsley leaves, chopped

¹⁄₄ cup fresh lemon juice

8 anchovy fillets, drained and mashed

¹⁄₂ red pepper, roasted (jarred is OK), chopped

2 shallots, finely chopped

1 tablespoon balsamic vinegar

1 clove garlic, chopped

³⁄₄ cup extra-virgin olive oil

1¹⁄₂ tablespoons drained capers

1 teaspoon grated lemon peel

Salt

Freshly ground pepper

Deglaze pot from veal with vinegar. Add parsley, lemon juice, anchovy fillets, roasted red peppers, shallots, and garlic, and mix. Whisk in olive oil. Add capers, lemon peel, salt, and pepper. Serve over veal.

Marla Mendelsohn

Carrot Soup

Heat oil in a large pot. Add carrot, onion, celery, potato, garlic, and sugar. Cover and cook over low heat for about 10 minutes, stirring occasionally.

Add the cloves, pepper, and broth and bring to a boil. Lower the heat and cook partially covered for about 20 minutes, until vegetables are soft.

Puree soup in processor and serve.

Marla Mendelsohn

2 teaspoons vegetable oil

1 pound carrots, sliced thin

1 large onion, chopped

$^2/_3$ cup celery, chopped

1$^1/_2$ cups peeled potato, diced

1 clove garlic, minced

$^1/_2$ teaspoon sugar

4 whole cloves

Freshly ground pepper to taste

4 cups chicken broth

Chocolate Soufflé

8 ounces semisweet chocolate, chopped

1 tablespoon butter

1 tablespoon flour

⅓ cup milk

3 egg yolks

1 teaspoon vanilla

4 egg whites

⅛ teaspoon cream of tartar

⅓ cup sugar

3 tablespoons confectioners' sugar, optional for garnish

Eight 6-ounce soufflé cups

Preheat oven to 375°F. Butter soufflé cups and sprinkle with sugar.

Melt chocolate over simmering water, stirring occasionally.

Melt butter in small saucepan. Add flour and cook for about 1 minute, stirring. Add milk, whisking briskly over medium heat, until mixture forms a smooth sauce. Continue cooking and whisking until sauce thickens, about 1 to 2 more minutes. Off heat, whisk in egg yolks and vanilla. Add this mixture to the melted chocolate and whisk until combined. Set aside.

Beat egg whites with cream of tartar until soft peaks form. Gradually sprinkle in sugar and continue to beat at high speed until stiff, but not dry. Fold ¼ whites into chocolate mixture to lighten and then fold in the remaining whites.

Fill individual soufflé dishes with mixture about ¾ up the sides. (You can refrigerate the soufflés at this point to be baked the next day.)

Bake on a cookie sheet for about 15 to 17 minutes. (A toothpick inserted should come out moist, but not gooey or runny.) Soufflés will puff and crack before they are done. Remove from the oven. Sprinkle with confectioners' sugar and serve with sweetened whipped cream.

Whipped Cream

1 cup heavy cream

1 teaspoon vanilla

2 to 3 teaspoons confectioners' sugar

Beat heavy cream with vanilla until thickened. Add confectioners' sugar and continue beating until peaks form.

Marla Mendelsohn, Adapted from Alice Medrich

DIANA ALBANESE comes from a family that has owned a food market in Bayonne, NJ, for 75 years. She has been a private caterer and was director of La Cucina D'ana. Diana studied at the French Culinary Institute, La Technique, and is on the faculty of Brookdale Community College's Creative Cooking Classes. **CAROLE WALTER**, Certified Culinary Professional, is author of *Great Cakes*, a James Beard Award-winning cookbook. A consultant and teacher, she has appeared on many major network television shows. Carole studied patisserie and culinary arts in Austria, Denmark, France, and Italy.

Italian Comfort Food

Diana Albanese

Carole Walter

Osso Buco with Cannellini Beans (ABOVE)

Mashed Potatoes with Parmesan Cheese, Drizzled Olive Oil, and Fried Sage Leaves

Sautéed Baby Spinach

Roasted Pear, Prosciutto, Parmesan, and Arugula Salad with Honey Vinaigrette (LEFT)

A Great Italian Cheesecake

Osso Buco with Cannellini Beans

Serves 6

Set rack on the lowest shelf and preheat oven to 350°F.

Dry shanks with paper towels and season with salt and pepper. Lightly dust with Wondra. Heat oil and butter in a large Dutch oven. Brown on all sides. This will take about 15 minutes. Remove shanks and set aside.

Add onion, carrots, and celery. Cook until softened, about 10 minutes.

Add wine, turning the heat up, and scrape the bottom of the pot to loosen the brown bits.

Add stock, tomatoes, and bay leaf. Return shanks to the pot and bring to a simmer. Cover and place in the oven. Cook for 2 hours, turning the shanks every half hour. Add more stock or water, if necessary.

When shanks are tender, remove from oven and set aside in a platter covered with foil.

Place Dutch oven over a burner set on medium heat. Add the cannellini beans and reduce the sauce to desired consistency.

Add the lemon zest, garlic, and parsley to the sauce. Taste for seasonings and adjust.

Serve sauce over veal shanks with risotto, mashed potatoes, or pasta.

NOTE: Soak the beans overnight in a large bowl or pot. Drain the beans and set in a large pot covered with water. Cover and bring to a boil. Reduce heat to a simmer and cook for 1 hour or until tender. Beans can be made several days ahead and kept refrigerated in their cooking liquids.

Diana Albanese

Osso Buco with Cannellini Beans is the perfect make ahead for comfortable entertaining. Add the fresh flavor of the "gremolata," the minced lemon zest, garlic, and parsley, just before serving.

Ingredients

Six 2-inch-thick pieces veal shanks

½ cup Wondra

2 tablespoons olive oil

2 tablespoons butter

1 medium onion, chopped medium fine

2 medium carrots, chopped medium fine

1 stalk celery, chopped medium fine

1 cup dry white wine

1 cup homemade or canned beef stock

One 28-ounce can Italian plum tomatoes roughly chopped by hand

2 bay leaves

2 cups cooked cannellini beans (white kidney beans); see note

1 tablespoon lemon zest

1 medium garlic clove, minced

2 tablespoons parsley, minced

Mashed Potatoes with Parmesan Cheese, Drizzled Olive Oil, and Fried Sage Leaves

Serves 8

2 pounds medium red boiling potatoes, choose older ones

6 to 8 tablespoons butter

1 cup milk or more if needed, hot

1 cup Parmesan cheese, freshly grated

Salt and freshly ground white pepper

10 sage leaves

Extra-virgin olive oil

This version of mashed potatoes with the fried sage leaves is especially nice with the sauce from the Osso Buco.

Place potatoes in a large saucepan and cover with water. Bring to a boil and cover the pan. Cook over medium heat until fork tender, about 30 minutes.

While the potatoes are cooking, place enough oil in a small skillet to come up to ½ inch up its sides. Turn the heat to high. When the oil is quite hot, slip in the sage and cook until crisp and slightly colored. Drain on paper towels and season with salt and pepper. Crumble when cooled.

When the potatoes are tender, set up a double boiler with simmering water. Set the butter into the top half to melt.

Drain the potatoes well and mash them through a food mill set over the melted butter. Using a whisk, beat the potatoes and slowly add the hot milk. After adding half the milk, beat in the grated cheese. When the cheese is well combined into the potatoes, continue adding the milk. When the potatoes will absorb no more milk, stop adding it. Taste for seasoning.

Add the sage to the potatoes. Serve the potatoes at once with a drizzle of the oil in which the leaves were fried.

Diana Albanese

Sautéed Baby Spinach

Serves 4

Two 10-ounce bags of fresh baby spinach

4 ounces unsalted butter, cut up

Salt and freshly ground black pepper to taste

Remove any long stems from the spinach. Rinse the spinach in water.

Place a large sauté pan over medium high heat. When the pan is hot, add the wet spinach. Cover and cook until the spinach is wilted, about 2 to 3 minutes.

Uncover; add the butter and salt and pepper. Stir to blend and serve immediately.

Diana Albanese

Roasted Pear, Prosciutto, Parmesan, and Arugula Salad with Honey Vinaigrette

Serves 8

Preheat oven to 400°F.

Grease a metal pan with 1 tablespoon of butter. Peel, cut in half, and core the pears. Place pears cut-side-down in pan. Sprinkle with sugar and dot with remaining butter. Bake for 25 minutes or longer, depending on the ripeness of the pears. Pears should be tender and caramelized. Remove from oven to cool slightly. Fan each pear half and set aside.

Arrange greens on each salad plate. Place endive on top. Arrange fanned pears on top of salad and evenly nap with vinaigrette. Drape prosciutto around the edges of the salad and top with cheese shavings. Top with freshly ground black pepper and serve.

Diana Albanese

2 tablespoons butter

4 medium ripe pears, Bartlett or Bosc

4 teaspoons sugar

2 bunches of arugula, washed, dried, and stems removed

2 heads endive chiffonade

1 recipe honey vinaigrette (recipe follows)

1/4 pound thinly sliced prosciutto

1 cup Parmesan shavings

Freshly ground black pepper

Honey Vinaigrette

Makes 3/4 Cup

Combine vinegar and honey in a bowl. Slowly whisk in oil. Season to taste and drizzle over salad greens.

Diana Albanese

1/4 cup balsamic vinegar

1 tablespoon honey

1/2 teaspoon garlic, finely minced

1/2 cup olive oil

Salt and freshly ground black pepper

These caramelized pears would be perfect with just about anything, but this salad combination is sure to become your favorite! Use a vegetable peeler to make the Parmesan cheese shavings.

A Great Italian Cheesecake

CRUMB CRUST

18 Amaretti biscuits, broken into pieces

2 tablespoons unflavored dried breadcrumbs

3 tablespoons unsalted butter, melted and cooled

CAKE

3 pounds fresh whole-milk ricotta

1 medium-size navel orange (about 6 ounces), washed and dried

8 large eggs

2 cups strained confectioners' sugar

3 tablespoons all-purpose flour

2 teaspoons vanilla extract

1/4 teaspoon salt

2/3 cup heavy cream

To extract excess water from the ricotta, arrange 2 linen or 100 percent cotton dish towels (do not use terrycloth) on top of each other on the kitchen counter. Spread the cheese lengthwise on the doubled towels into a rectangle measuring about 14 × 5 inches. Bring the sides of the towels to the center and roll the cheese tightly in the towels, jelly-roll fashion. Let the cheese stand for a half hour. Unroll the towels and replace them with two clean, dry towels. Repeat the procedure, letting the cheese stand for another half hour.

Butter a 9-inch springform pan.

To make the crust, add the biscuits and the bread crumbs to the bowl of a food processor fitted with the steel blade. Pulse 6 to 8 times or until fine crumbs form. You should have 3/4 cup crumbs. Stop the machine and pour in the melted butter. Pulse 3 times just to blend.

Empty the crumb mixture into the prepared pan. With the bottom of a glass, press the crumbs evenly onto the bottom of the pan. (Do not extend the crumbs up the sides.) Refrigerate while you prepare the filling.

Position rack in the lower third of the oven. Preheat the oven to 325°F.

To make the cake, cut the entire orange, including rind and pith, into 2-inch chunks. You should have about 2 cups. Place the eggs and orange chunks into the bowl of a food processor fitted with the steel blade. Process for 2 minutes, until the mixture is thick and light in color and the orange pieces are finely chopped.

Stop the machine and add the ricotta and all of the remaining ingredients except the heavy cream. The volume of the ingredients will reduce in mixing. Process for 10 seconds, or just until smooth and creamy. Scrape down the sides and process for 5 seconds longer.

With the machine running, pour in the cream through the feeder tube. Immediately pour the filling into the pan.

Set the pan on a 12-inch square of aluminum foil, molding the foil around the sides of the pan to catch leakage. In the preheated oven, bake for 70 to 75 minutes, or until the top of the cake is golden brown. Turn off the heat and prop the oven door ajar with the handle of a wooden spoon. Cool the cake in the oven for an additional half hour.

Remove the cake from the oven. Set the pan on a cake rack to cool completely. Refrigerate at least 3 to 4 hours to set. Remove the cake from the refrigerator at least 1 hour before serving. Run a thin knife around the sides of the pan and carefully remove the rim.

The cake can be stored, refrigerated, covered loosely with aluminum foil, for up to 1 week.

Carole Walter

DANIEL C. ROSATI is owner of La Villa Cucina, a cooking school in the Tuscany region of Italy. He also teaches at the New School for Social Research in New York and various other schools around the country. His work with several noted chefs includes a position as teaching assistant to Giuliano Bugialli. A member of the IACP, Daniel's specialties include regional Italian cooking, Middle Eastern cooking, and pastry arts.

Fish—A European Christmas Tradition

Daniel C. Rosati

3-Grain Calamari Fritti

Cacciucco

Shrimp Santorini Style (ABOVE)

Portugese Style "Clams Casino" (LEFT)

Double Caramel Crème Brûlée (OPPOSITE PAGE)

137

3-Grain Calamari Fritti

1½ pounds cleaned squid, cut into ½-inch rings

1 egg

½ cup milk

1 cup flour

1 cup rice flour

1 cup Graham cracker crumbs

Salt

Pepper

6 cups safflower oil

DIPPING SAUCE

¼ cup olive oil

1 garlic clove, minced

2 anchovy fillets

½ teaspoon cayenne pepper

½ teaspoon chili powder

½ teaspoon paprika

1 teaspoon Dijon mustard

1 teaspoon capers

1 cup mayonnaise

½ cup sour cream

Pepper

Combine the milk and the egg in a medium size bowl; whisk until well blended. Add the squid pieces and refrigerate until needed.

Combine the flour, rice flour, and Graham crumbs in a small bowl. Season with salt and pepper.

Combine the ingredients for the dipping sauce in the bowl of a food processor. Pulse 4 or 5 times until well blended. Season with pepper. Place in a small bowl and refrigerate until needed.

Heat the oil in a frying pan until the temperature reaches 350°F.

Dredge the squid pieces in the seasoned grain mixture. Fry in small batches until well browned all over.

Serve hot with prepared dipping sauce.

Daniel C. Rosati

Cacciucco

Tuscan Fish Stew from Livorno

Serves 8

Heat the oil in a large Dutch oven over medium heat, add the onion, carrot, celery, and fennel. Sauté until tender, then add the garlic. Continue to sauté 1 minute longer, then add the wine. Cook for 3 minutes or until most of the wine has evaporated. Add the tomato puree, bay leaves, red pepper, and parsley. Cover pot and allow to simmer for 20 minutes. Season well with salt and pepper. Add the broth and seafood; cook until clams and mussels have fully opened, about 15 minutes. To serve, place a piece of toasted bread in a deep soup bowl, ladle stew over bread with plenty of broth. Garnish with a drizzle of olive oil and chopped parsley.

Daniel C. Rosati

⅓ cup olive oil

1 large red onion, chopped

1 large carrot, diced

1 celery rib, diced

1 stem fresh fennel, minced

4 garlic cloves, minced

½ cup red wine

32 ounces tomato puree

2 bay leaves

½ teaspoon crushed red pepper

15 sprigs Italian parsley, leaves only, chopped

Salt

Pepper

1 cup fish broth

1 pound halibut fillets, cubed

1 pound sea scallops

1 pound peeled and deveined shrimp

1 pound cleaned squid, cut into rings

1 pound scrubbed and debearded mussels

24 mahogany clams or cockles

8 large slices rustic Italian bread, toasted then rubbed with 1 large peeled garlic clove

⅓ cup olive oil (for garnish)

20 sprigs Italian parsley, leaves only, chopped

Shrimp Santorini Style

½ cup olive oil

¼ teaspoon red pepper flakes

1 bay leaf

5 garlic cloves, chopped

4 ripe tomatoes, diced

Salt

Pepper

8 colossal shrimp, peeled and deveined (12 to 15 count)

1 tablespoon olive oil

8 ounces crumbled Feta cheese

1 teaspoon Greek oregano

Heat ½ cup olive oil in a large sauté pan over medium heat. When oil is hot add the red pepper flakes, bay leaf, and garlic. Sauté for 2 minutes, add the tomatoes, and sauté for an additional 2 minutes. Remove from heat and season well with salt and pepper.

Place the shrimp in a lightly oiled gratin. Drizzle the shrimp with 1 tablespoon olive oil. Season shrimp lightly with salt and pepper.

Pour the tomato mixture over the shrimp. Top with crumbled Feta and oregano. Bake on the top shelf of a preheated 400°F. oven for 20 minutes.

Daniel C. Rosati

Portuguese Style "Clams Casino"

Serves 8

Heat the oil in a small sauté pan, when oil is hot add the garlic and peppers. Sauté for 4 minutes. Remove from heat and season with salt and pepper.

Place the clams on a jelly-roll pan, top each with a spoonful of the pepper mixture, then top each with a slice of chorizo.

Preheat oven to 425°F. Bake for about 10 minutes.

Daniel C. Rosati

2 dozen littleneck clams, steamed open, empty shell removed

⅓ cup olive oil

3 garlic cloves, minced

1 red pepper, minced

1 green pepper, minced

Salt

Pepper

2 links chorizo sausage, sliced into 24 thin slices

Double Caramel Crème Brûlée

Eight 6-ounce ramekins

1 cup *dulce de leche*

3 cups heavy cream

1 cup milk

½ cup sugar

4 eggs

4 egg yolks

1 vanilla bean, split

Granulated sugar

Place 2 tablespoons of *dulce de leche* in the bottom of each ramekin. Place ramekins in a roasting pan.

Preheat oven to 350°F.

In a medium size sauce pan, combine the heavy cream, milk, and vanilla bean. Heat over low flame until mixture reaches a simmer. Cool slightly then scrape inside pulp of vanilla bean and discard.

In a medium size bowl, combine eggs, egg yolks, and sugar. Beat until light and fluffy.

Slowly pour warm milk mixture into egg mixture and stir until well combined.

Return the mixture to the saucepan and stir over low heat until "custard" is thick enough to lightly coat a spoon.

Pour mixture into ramekins and pour hot water into roasting pan to create a water bath. Place roasting pan in oven and bake until custards are set, about 30 minutes.

Remove from oven and water bath. Cool completely!

Before serving, sprinkle each with sugar. Torch tops with the aid of a small butane torch to caramelize sugar.

Daniel C. Rosati

Every country seems to have its own version of a sweet creamy custard—the flan, crème anglaise, panna cotta. This crème brûlée gets its caramel on both top and bottom with the addition of *dulce de leche*.

JOAN D'AMICO, a former home economics teacher, hold a Masters Degree in child development and family relationships. She's an educational consultant in Bergen County, NJ, freelances for several major food companies, and conducts cooking workshops in elementary schools. Joan has recently published her third children's book, *The Healthy Body Cookbook*.

Approaching Vegetarianism

Joan D'Amico

Wild Mushroom Strudels

Roasted Vegetable Cassoulet (ABOVE)

Spicy Cornbread

Chocolate Almond Torte (LEFT)

143

Wild Mushroom Strudels

8 ounces shiitake mushrooms, destemmed and sliced

4 ounces domestic mushrooms, sliced

$\frac{1}{3}$ cup shallots, chopped (approximately 2 large)

2 cloves garlic, chopped

3 tablespoons olive oil

$\frac{1}{3}$ cup Madeira

$\frac{1}{3}$ to $\frac{1}{2}$ cup cream

2 teaspoons fresh thyme

Salt and pepper to taste

4 sheets phyllo

4 to 5 tablespoons melted butter

Thyme sprigs

It's always a trick to make a vegetarian meal that meat eaters will love as well. The key is mushrooms. Wild mushrooms and Madeira wine team up to make a rich filling for a Wild Mushroom Strudel.

Prepare all vegetables. Heat a 12-inch skillet, add oil and shallots, and sauté 1 minute. Add mushrooms and garlic and saute 2 to 3 minutes, deglaze the pan with Madeira, and reduce until almost no liquid remains.

Add cream, thyme, and seasoning to the mushrooms and reduce until thick. Let mixture cool slightly.

Prepare phyllo by brushing each layer with butter (place each buttered layer on top of the next). Cut the phyllo in half width-wise, cut each half into three squares (approximately $\frac{1}{2} \times 5\frac{1}{2}$ inches). Place each square into a well-buttered muffin tin, overlapping the edges.

Place 2 heaping tablespoons of filling on each square and fold over overlapping edges. Brush top with butter and repeat with remaining squares. Bake strudels in a preheated 400°F. oven for 18 to 20 minutes, remove from muffin tin, and bake for 4 more minutes. Garnish with a sprig of thyme.

Joan D'Amico

Roasted Vegetable Cassoulet

Serves 6

Preheat the oven to 350°F.

Toss the fennel, leeks, mushrooms, and carrot with ½ teaspoon salt, ¼ teaspoon pepper, and 1 tablespoon olive oil. Put the vegetables in a large roasting pan and roast until they begin to brown, about 45 minutes.

Meanwhile, combine the remaining salt, pepper, olive oil, and thyme. Divide this mixture in half and toss the shallots with one-half. Place in a small flameproof baking dish and cover. Bake alongside the vegetables. Toss the garlic with the other half of the oil mixture. After 20 minutes, uncover the shallots and add the garlic to that dish. Continue to bake uncovered until both shallots and garlic are soft and brown, about 10 minutes.

Remove the shallots and garlic from the baking dish and set aside. Deglaze the pan by adding ¼ cup of the stock and, using a wooden spoon, scrape up the bits that are stuck to the bottom. Set aside until the vegetables finish roasting.

Add the shallots, garlic, beans, and ¼ cup of the parsley to the roasted vegetables. Stir in the remaining ¼ cup stock and the reserved shallot-onion glaze. Put all of the vegetables into a 2-quart ovenproof casserole.

Combine the butter, remaining ¼ cup parsley, cheese, and bread crumbs in a bowl and sprinkle over the cassoulet.

Bake for 30 minutes, or until the bread crumbs are brown and the beans are hot.

Joan D'Amico

½ medium fennel bulb, cut vertically into ½-inch thick pieces

2 medium leeks, white and green parts, cleaned and cut into 1-inch pieces

1 large portobella mushroom or 3 shiitake mushrooms, cut into 1-inch slices

1 unpeeled carrot, cut into 1-inch pieces

1½ teaspoons salt

¾ teaspoon freshly ground black pepper

2 tablespoons olive oil

1 teaspoon dried thyme

6 peeled shallots

6 garlic cloves, split

1 cup vegetable stock

2½ cups canned cannellini beans

½ cup fresh parsley, chopped

2 tablespoons butter

⅓ cup grated Parmesan cheese

½ cup bread crumbs

This Roasted Vegetable Cassoulet gets its heartiness from portobella mushrooms and cannellini beans.

Spicy Cornbread

1 cup stone ground yellow cornmeal

1 cup all-purpose flour

2 tablespoons sugar

1 tablespoon baking powder

1 teaspoon salt

½ teaspoon baking soda

¾ cup buttermilk

3 large eggs

4 tablespoons unsalted butter, melted

¼ teaspoon cayenne pepper

Preheat the oven to 450°F. Grease and line an 8 × 8 × 2-inch pan with parchment paper.

Combine all the dry ingredients in a mixing bowl and stir well.

In a separate bowl, whisk the buttermilk and eggs together. Quickly whisk in the melted butter.

Stir the liquids into the dry ingredients and avoid overmixing.

Spread the batter into a prepared pan and smooth out the top.

Bake the cornbread for approximately 20 to 25 minutes. Cool and serve with butter.

Joan D'Amico

Chocolate Almond Torte

Serves 6

Preheat the oven to 350°F. Butter a 10-inch round springform cake pan. Dust the bottom and the sides of the pan with sugar, tapping out the excess.

Melt the chocolate in a bowl set over a pan of simmering water. Set aside and allow to cool for 2 to 3 minutes.

Whip the butter with ½ cup of the sugar in a mixer until very light and fluffy, about 5 minutes. Beat in the egg yolks and melted chocolate. In a separate bowl, whip egg whites until light and frothy. Gradually add the remaining ⅓ cup sugar and beat until the egg whites are stiff. Fold in ½ cup almonds, vanilla, and ⅓ egg white mixture into the chocolate mixture; then fold in the remaining whites. Pour the batter into the pan and bake for 30 to 40 minutes. Cool completely and unmold.

Evenly spread entire cake with ganache and garnish with chopped and whole almonds.

6 ounces semisweet chocolate, chopped

1½ sticks unsalted butter

⅔ cup sugar

8 eggs, separated

½ cup plus two teaspoons chopped blanched almonds

1 teaspoon vanilla extract

Ganache

Whole almonds for garnishing

Ganache

Heat cream over medium heat until very hot, but not boiling. Place chocolate in a bowl. Pour hot cream over the chocolate. Mix with a spatula until smooth. Use warm as a glaze, or cool. Store in an airtight container in the refrigerator for up to 1 week.

Joan D'Amico

8 ounces cream

8 ounces semisweet chocolate

End the meal with this thin rich chocolate cake and everyone will forget about the meat. When you stir the ganache, stir gently and try not to incorporate any air bubbles. Quickly pour it over the cake and, with a few quick strokes, you will be done. Excessive fussing can cause streaks to appear after it sets.

ARLENE SARAPPO studied Italian cooking in Bologna, Florence, Venice, and Sicily with Marcella Hazan and Giuliano Bugialli. She is the former manager of cooking studios at Kings. Arlene is a member of the IACP, a trustee of the NJ Agricultural Society, and executive vice president of NYACP.

Easy and Elegant Dinner Party

Arlene Sarappo

Roast Tenderloin of Beef with a Red Wine and Shallot Sauce (OPPOSITE PAGE)

Gratin Dauphinoise

Watercress and Endive Salad with a Walnut Vinaigrette

Chocolate Passion (LEFT)

Crème Anglaise

Roast Tenderloin of Beef with a Red Wine and Shallot Sauce

Serves 6 to 8

1 fully trimmed and tied tenderloin of beef, prime or choice, at room temperature

1 tablespoon olive oil

When making the Red Wine and Shallot Sauce, don't be afraid to reduce the wine. It concentrates the flavor. And when you swirl in the cold butter just before serving, remove it from the heat first—it shouldn't boil, because it will break down.

Preheat oven to 400°F.

Brush the roast all over with olive oil.

Set ridged side up in a shallow roasting pan and place in the upper third of your oven. After about 8 minutes, turn and brush with a bit more oil. At the end of 30 minutes, sprinkle with salt and pepper and check internal temperature with an instant meat thermometer. For very rare, remove from oven at 120°F. For medium rare, remove from oven at 125°F., and for medium, remove at 130°F. to 135°F. Total cooking time should be between 35 and 45 minutes.

Remove meat from oven at desired temperature and set on a warm platter. Cover loosely with foil. Allow to sit at room temperature for 15 to 20 minutes before carving. This resting period is most important—the juices will be reabsorbed by the roast as it sits and the meat will continue to cook; in fact, the internal temperature will rise 7 to 10 degrees during the resting period.

Arlene Sarappo

Red Wine and Shallot Sauce

Serves 8

6 tablespoons shallots, minced

6 black peppercorns, crushed

1½ cups high quality dry red wine

2 cups demi-glace

Salt

Freshly ground pepper

4 tablespoons cold butter

Combine in a small, heavy saucepan the shallots, peppercorns, and red wine. Bring to boil over high heat. Reduce heat to medium and simmer until the liquid is reduced to a glaze (about ¼ of the original amount will be left).

Add the demi-glace, bring to a boil, lower heat a bit, and reduce to thicken slightly. Taste; season with salt and pepper. Strain. Sauce can be made to this point several hours ahead and stored in the refrigerator.

At serving time, reheat. Remove from heat, swirl in the cold butter, and serve.

Arlene Sarappo

Gratin Dauphinoise

Serves 8

Rich and luxurious, the gratin dauphinoise is a classic French accompaniment to roast meats. Variations are as many as there are cooks.

Preheat oven to 400°F.

Peel and rinse potatoes. Slice about ⅛ inch thick. This can be done in a food processor, using the slicing blade and applying light pressure. Put potato slices in a 3-quart saucepan. Pour on just enough milk to barely cover the potatoes. Add the garlic cloves. Place over moderate heat and bring to a boil. Add 1½ teaspoons salt. Reduce heat and simmer for 12 minutes. Drain into a colander. Discard the garlic.

Butter a shallow ovenproof dish; use an 11-inch fluted porcelain quiche dish. Be sure to choose a dish with a large surface area, so that at serving time each guest can be served a portion that contains the browned top.

Arrange a slightly overlapping layer of potato slices on the bottom of the dish. Season with salt and pepper. Sprinkle with ⅓ cup of the Gruyère. Top with ¼ cup cream. Repeat layering 2 additional times to form a total of 3 layers.

Bake on a foil-lined cookie sheet placed in the upper third of the oven, until the gratin is golden brown and bubbly, about 40 to 45 minutes. Let settle for a few minutes and then serve immediately.

Arlene Sarappo

2½ pounds Yukon gold potatoes

Milk, enough to barely cover the potatoes when placed in a 3-quart saucepan

3 large garlic cloves

1 tablespoon butter

Salt

Freshly ground pepper

¾ cup heavy cream

¾ to 1 cup Gruyère cheese, freshly grated

Watercress and Endive Salad with a Walnut Vinaigrette

Serves 4

DRESSING

3 tablespoons lemon juice

1 heaping teaspoon Dijon mustard

¼ cup tasteless vegetable oil

¼ cup walnut oil

Salt and pepper to taste

SALAD

1 bag watercress, stems removed, rinsed, and spun dry

2 large Belgian endives

¼ cup walnut pieces, toasted in a 350°F. oven for 10 minutes

Prepare dressing by combining lemon juice and mustard in a large mixing bowl. Whisk to mix well. Combine the oils and slowly whisk in the lemon and mustard mixture. Season with salt and pepper. Set aside or refrigerate for longer storage.

Just before serving, remove outer leaves from the endives and discard. Slice endives horizontally into slices about ¼-inch thick. Place in a large salad bowl along with the watercress and walnuts. Spoon on just enough dressing to lightly coat the greens. Toss well. Arrange on salad plates.

Serve immediately.

Arlene Sarappo

Chocolate Passion

Dense, dark, and deliciously chocolate, this cake is bound to please any chocolate lover. It is easy to prepare and can be made a few days in advance. In fact, its flavor will improve as it ages. Because it is rather plain looking, serve it as a plated dessert. Its adornment can be as simple as a dollop of whipped cream with a few raspberries scattered about. Delicious, but a bit more time consuming, would be to set each slice atop a pool of crème anglaise.

Preheat oven to 350°F.

Grease the bottom and sides of a 9-inch springform pan with butter. Line the bottom with a circle of parchment paper. Butter the paper. Set aside.

Combine the chocolate, butter, and coffee in the top of a double boiler. Set over simmering water. Stir occasionally until melted and smooth. Remove from heat and cool slightly.

Whisk the egg yolks into the chocolate mixture. Sift the sugar and cocoa into the chocolate mixture. Whisk to blend. Set aside.

Place egg whites in a large, clean bowl. Add a pinch of salt. With an electric beater, beat until the whites hold a soft peak. Gently whisk 1/3 of the beaten egg whites into the chocolate mixture. Use a large rubber spatula to fold in the remaining egg whites. Be careful not to overmix. Pour the batter into the prepared pan and place on the lower middle rack of the preheated oven. Bake for 30 minutes.

Remove cake from oven and place on a wire rack to cool. Loosen, but do not remove the collar of the springform pan. Allow the cake to cool completely.

Remove the collar from the cooled cake and invert cake onto a serving plate. Remove the bottom of the springform pan and carefully peel away the parchment.

If you are preparing the cake a few days in advance, cover loosely with foil wrap and refrigerate. Bring back to room temperature before serving.

Arlene Sarappo

7 ounces imported bittersweet chocolate

7 ounces unsalted butter

2 tablespoons prepared espresso (instant espresso is fine)

5 large eggs, separated

1/2 cup granulated sugar

2 tablespoons Dutch processed cocoa

Pinch of salt

Crème Anglaise

Makes Approximately 1½ Cups

Crème anglaise or custard sauce is the base for a number of classics including ice cream and pastry cream. It is not difficult to make but requires your undivided attention.

1 cup whole milk

¼ cup granulated sugar

3 large egg yolks

1 teaspoon vanilla extract

Set a sieve atop a medium size mixing bowl. Set aside; you will later use this to strain the sauce.

Combine the milk and 2 tablespoons of the sugar in a heavy-bottomed saucepan. Adjust heat to medium and bring the mixture just to a boil.

While the milk is heating, place the yolks in a medium size mixing bowl. Whisk to combine and add the remaining sugar. Whisk until the yolks ribbon.

If you don't have the time to make the Crème Anglaise, just melt some high quality vanilla ice cream. It's an easy way out!

Pour about half of the heated milk into the yolk mixture, whisking continuously until they are combined. Pour the mixture back into the saucepan, whisk to combine, and return to medium low heat. Stir constantly with a wooden spoon until the mixture thickens slightly and coats a spoon. As it approaches readiness, you will see steam rise from the pan and white foam at the surface will disappear. Do not bring to a boil or the eggs will curdle. Remove from the heat and strain. Stir in vanilla. Let cool for about 10 minutes, stirring from time to time. Then cover and refrigerate. As the sauce chills, it will continue to thicken. Crème anglaise can be prepared up to 3 days in advance. Be sure that it is covered tightly, so that it does not absorb your refrigerator's odors.

Variation: Add the zest of one orange to the milk while it is heating. Remove zest before adding the heated milk to the yolks. Add 1 tablespoon of orange liqueur along with the vanilla to the finished sauce.

Arlene Sarappo

MARLA MENDELSOHN, Certified Culinary professional, is owner of Cook Ease catering and event planning. She teaches culinary arts in the New Jersey–New York area with a focus on multigenerational programs, and also serves as a product development consultant to food companies. Marla studied at the Ritz Escoffier, Paris, and is a member of the IACP and NYACP. She is the creator of a children's cooking video, *Kids Can Cook*.

Breaking the Fast

Marla Mendelsohn

Mediterranean Vegetable and Goat Cheese Terrine

Mustard Crusted Salmon with Shallot Vinaigrette (LEFT)

Spinach Soufflé with Red Pepper Sauce

Scallion Pancakes (ABOVE)

Roasted Shiitake, Asparagus, and Onion Confit Frittata

Sour Cream Streusel Cake

155

Mediterranean Vegetable and Goat Cheese Terrine

Serves 12

6 red peppers, halved and seeded

6 yellow peppers, halved and seeded

3 tablespoons olive oil

1 large eggplant, peeled and cut into 7 slices, 1/4-inch thick

2 1/2 pounds goat cheese

2 lemons, zested

2 tablespoons garlic, minced

2 tablespoons chives, chopped

3 sprigs basil for garnish

Cooking oil

Roast peppers under broiler until completely charred. Place in bag to steam and cool. Peel charred skin and slice into julienne strips. Season with salt and pepper.

Sauté eggplant slices in hot oil over medium high heat until golden. Season with salt and pepper.

Combine cheese, garlic, lemon zest, and chives.

Spray a 6-to-8-cup terrine with cooking oil. Alternate layers of red and yellow peppers, cheese, and eggplant, beginning and ending with peppers. Refrigerate overnight. Unmold and slice. Serve garnished with a basil leaf.

Marla Mendelsohn

It's worth the effort to roast your own peppers; the flavor is far superior to any you can buy. Just make sure they are completely charred all over. They only need to cool enough for you to handle them. They can also be done a day or two ahead.

Mustard Crusted Salmon with Shallot Vinaigrette

Serves 6

Mix mustard, matzah meal, egg white, and butter. Set aside.

Season both sides of salmon with salt and pepper. Add 2 tablespoons olive oil to hot sauté pan. Sauté each piece of salmon on 1 side only for about 1 minute. Remove from pan and cool.

Coat seared surfaces of salmon with ⅛ inch thick layer of mustard mixture (mixture will be thick).

Sauté mushroom caps in moderately hot sauté pan with 3 tablespoon of olive oil, until browned on all sides and cooked through, about 4 minutes. Season with salt and pepper and keep warm.

Heat 2 tablespoons of olive oil in sauté pan. Place salmon mustard-side-down in hot sauté pan and, after about 30 seconds (crust is lightly browned), flip salmon and cook 30 seconds more. Place salmon in 350°F. oven for 5 to 8 minutes, until slightly medium rare in center.

Caramelized Shallot Vinaigrette

Heat 3 tablespoons of oil in a sauté pan and sauté 1 cup of shallots until lightly browned. Combine cooked shallots and remaining ingredients in a food processor and puree until smooth. If too thick, add water as necessary.

Place mushrooms on serving platter. Place salmon fillets over mushrooms. Spoon vinaigrette around salmon and sprinkle with parsley.

Marla Mendelsohn

⅓ cup Dijon mustard

1 cup matzah meal

1 egg white

Salt

Freshly ground pepper

4 tablespoons butter or margarine

Four 6-ounce pieces salmon, sliced 1 inch thick, skin removed

7 tablespoons olive oil

4 medium portobella mushroom caps

2 tablespoons parsley, finely chopped

1 cup plus 1 tablespoon sliced, peeled shallot

11 tablespoons extra-virgin olive oil

2 tablespoons sherry vinegar

2 tablespoons balsamic vinegar

¼ cup water

1 tablespoon Dijon mustard

1½ teaspoons salt

½ teaspoon white pepper

Spinach Soufflé with Red Pepper Sauce

Serves 4

Two 10-ounce packages frozen creamed spinach, thawed

¾ cup grated Swiss cheese, about 3 ounces

¼ teaspoon salt

¼ teaspoon pepper

2 egg yolks

3 egg whites

2 red peppers, halved and seeded

1 teaspoon balsamic vinegar

1 large shallot, coarsely chopped

Preheat oven to 400°F. Butter 9-inch glass pie plate.

Roast red peppers under broiler until skins are charred. Place in bag to steam and cool. When cool, peel off charred skins.

Blend creamed spinach, Swiss cheese, salt, and pepper. Whisk in egg yolks.

Beat egg whites until stiff, but not dry. Fold egg whites into spinach mixture. Gently pour into prepared pie plate. Bake until set, about 18 minutes.

Puree 1 roasted red pepper in food processor with vinegar until almost smooth. Add remaining red pepper and shallots and chop, pulsing, until a chunky puree forms. Transfer sauce to small saucepan and heat until warmed through; season with salt and pepper.

Spoon soufflé onto plates and top with red pepper sauce.

Marla Mendelsohn

Scallion Pancakes

Bring a medium pot of salted water to a boil.

Roughly chop 3 bunches scallions and mince 1 bunch scallions. Add the rough-cut scallions to the boiling water and cook for 5 minutes, until tender. Drain and reserve ½ cup liquid. Puree the scallions, adding some of the cooking liquid as needed.

Mix the scallion puree with the egg and soy sauce. Gently stir in the flour. Add pepper to taste and reserved minced scallions.

Pour a thin layer of oil into sauté pan and heat. Drop the batter by the tablespoonful or ¼ cup. Cook about 2 minutes on a side, until lightly browned.

NOTE: Pancakes can be kept warm in a 200°F. oven for about 30 minutes.

Marla Mendelsohn

4 bunches scallions

1 egg

1 teaspoon soy sauce

½ cup flour

Salt

Freshly ground pepper

Canola oil

Roasted Shiitake, Asparagus, and Onion Confit Frittata

Serves 6

8 shiitake mushrooms

Olive oil

Balsamic vinegar

10 asparagus spears

4 tablespoons red wine onion confit (see recipe below)

8 large eggs, beaten

4 tablespoons canola oil

½ cup grated Fontina cheese

2 tablespoons fresh thyme, minced

Preheat oven to 375°F. Brush shiitake mushrooms with olive oil, sprinkle with vinegar, salt and pepper to taste. Wrap in foil and roast for 20 minutes. Cool and cut into quarters.

Blanch asparagus in salted boiling water for 4 minutes. Plunge into ice bath. Drain and cut into ½-inch pieces.

Sauté onion confit, shiitake mushrooms, and asparagus in canola oil in nonstick ovenproof sauté pan for 1 minute. Add eggs and cook, stirring, for 1 minute. Place in 375°F. oven for 5 minutes, or until set. Slide onto serving platter and sprinkle with Fontina cheese and thyme.

Red Wine Onion Confit

2 onions, cut into julienne strips

2 tablespoons olive oil

1 cup red wine

½ cup port

½ cup sugar

Sauté onions in oil over medium high heat until soft. Add wine, port, and sugar and bring to a simmer. Cook over medium heat until liquid evaporates. Season with salt and pepper.

Marla Mendelsohn

Sour Cream Streusel Cake

Serves 8 to 10

Preheat oven to 350°F. Spray a 12-cup Bundt pan with cooking oil.

Mix nuts, brown sugar, cinnamon, and cocoa powder, and set aside. Sift flour, baking soda, baking powder, and salt together, and set aside.

Cream butter with 1½ cups sugar. Beat in eggs, one at a time. Mix in vanilla. Mix dry ingredients and sour cream alternately into butter mixture. Beat batter on high for 1 minute.

Pour ⅓ batter into prepared pan. Sprinkle with half of nut mixture. Spoon ⅓ of batter over top and sprinkle with remaining nut mixture. Finish it off with remaining batter.

Bake about 1 hour, until cake tester comes out clean. Cool cake in pan for 10 minutes on a rack. Cut around pan sides to loosen cake. Turn cake out onto rack and cool 1 hour. Transfer to a serving platter.

Whisk confectioners' sugar and milk until smooth. Drizzle over top of cake. Serve slightly warm or at room temperature.

Marla Mendelsohn

1¼ cups walnuts, coarsely chopped

1¼ cups light brown sugar

4½ teaspoons cinnamon

4½ teaspoons unsweetened cocoa powder

3 cups cake flour

1½ teaspoons baking soda

1½ teaspoons baking powder

¾ teaspoon salt

¾ cup butter, room temperature

1½ cups sugar

3 eggs

1 tablespoon vanilla

One 16-ounce container sour cream

1 cup confectioners' sugar

1 tablespoon milk

Cooking oil

STEVEN CAPODICASA, a graduate of the Culinary Institute of America, cooked for several U.S. presidents while working for the Hilton Hotel chain. Steve was head of new product development for Kings Super Markets. He presently serves on the advisory boards of numerous major food companies.

Valentine's Day Dinner

Steven Capodicasa

Shrimp and White Bean Bruschetta (LEFT)

Baby Greens Served with a Roasted Beet Vinaigrette

Lobster Risotto (ABOVE)

Warm Chocolate Cake

Shrimp and White Bean Bruschetta

Serves 6

1 loaf fresh Italian bread

2 cups cooked cannellini beans

2 dozen small shrimp (55 to 60 count), peeled and deveined

2 cups diced plum tomatoes, seeded and peeled

4 cloves garlic, minced

½ cup sweet vermouth

1 cup olive oil

½ cup fresh Italian parsley, chopped

¼ cup basil leaves, chiffonade

⅛ cup red wine vinegar

⅛ cup balsamic vinegar

Kosher salt to taste

Red pepper flakes to taste

Slice bread into large 3-inch bias cuts. Lightly brush bread with olive oil, place on a preheated grill, and grill on both sides.

Heat a sauté pan. Add ¼ cup olive oil and 1 tablespoon minced garlic. Add shrimp and sauté for 3 to 4 minutes. Deglaze with sweet vermouth. Chill.

Mix together cooked beans, shrimp, tomatoes, minced garlic, parsley, basil, ¾ cup olive oil, and vinegars. Toss and season with Kosher salt and pepper flakes.

Arrange grilled bread on a platter and top with shrimp mixture.

Steven Capodicasa

Baby Greens Served with a Roasted Beet Vinaigrette

Serves 6

Wash beets under cold water; wrap in foil and place in a preheated 450°F. oven. Roast for about 1 to 1¼ hours until fork pierces them easily. Cool and peel.

Place 1 cooked beet, garlic, and shallot in a blender. Process until smooth, adding oil and vinegar. Season with salt and pepper.

Finely julienne the last cooked beet for garnish. Arrange baby greens on a platter and garnish with beet and thinly sliced red onion.

Steven Capodicasa

12 ounces fresh baby greens

2 large fresh beets

1 shallot

2 cloves garlic

1 cup canola oil

⅓ cup apple cider vinegar

1 small red onion, sliced thin

Salt and pepper to taste

Lobster Risotto

3 tablespoons olive oil

½ cup onion, finely chopped

2 cloves garlic, minced

2 cups arborio rice

4 cups fish stock

1 cup white wine

12 ounces cooked lobster
meat, cut into large dice

1 tablespoon saffron

White pepper to taste

Kosher salt to taste

¼ stick sweet butter

½ cup Italian parsley, chopped

Heat olive oil in a heavy bottomed pot. Add diced onions, rice, and minced garlic; sauté slowly for 3 to 5 minutes. Heat stock.

Add in white wine, stirring until all of wine is absorbed. Add in ½ cup of stock and saffron; stir until all of stock is absorbed. Continue adding ½ cup of stock at a time until rice is tender.

Add in lobster meat and butter. Adjust seasoning with salt and pepper. Garnish with chopped parsley.

Steven Capodicasa

The preparation of arborio rice differs from the preparation of regular rice; you gradually add the liquid and it takes from 20 to 40 minutes (and constant attention), depending on the intensity of the heat and your taste. If you like arborio rice soft and creamy, stick to 40 minutes; al dente will be closer to 20 minutes. Be sure to keep the stock hot as you gradually add it to the rice. If you need additional liquid, use water.

Warm Chocolate Cake

1 pound bittersweet
chocolate, chopped

1½ pounds sweet butter

1½ pounds sugar

¾ pound all-purpose flour

1 dozen eggs

1 dozen egg yolks

½ teaspoon salt

1 teaspoon pure vanilla

12 small ramekins, lightly
buttered

12 medium chunks of
chocolate

Melt chocolate and butter over a double boiler, chill slightly, and whisk in sugar and flour.

Whisk in eggs and egg yolks a little at a time until all the eggs get incorporated. Add salt and vanilla extract.

Pour into ramekins. Insert one chocolate chunk into the middle of each cake. Bake for 8 to 10 minutes in a preheated 350°F. oven.

Steven Capodicasa

SPRING

KATHLEEN K. SANDERSON, a graduate of the California Culinary Institute, is Consulting Food Editor of *Restaurant Business* magazine. In addition, Kathleen serves as a consultant to several food companies.

Do Ahead
Santa Fe Buffet

Kathleen K. Sanderson

Jalapeño Poppers

Southwestern Strip Steaks (LEFT)

Guacamole

Salsa Cruda

Bitter Greens and Citrus Salad (ABOVE)

Mexican Wedding Cookies

Sangria (OPPOSITE PAGE)

Jalapeño Poppers

7 whole jalapeños, split and seeded

4 ounces cream cheese

4 ounces shredded cheddar cheese (1 cup)

¼ cup cilantro, chopped

1 cup flour

2 beaten eggs

2 cups dry cornbread or corn flake crumbs

Vegetable oil for frying

Sour Cream

Salsa

In a bowl combine cheeses and cilantro, mix well. Mound 1 tablespoon of cheese mixture in each jalapeño half and refrigerate until firm.

Dip stuffed jalapeños in flour, then in eggs and cover with crumbs. Refrigerate at least one hour.

Fill a high-sided pan or deep fryer about ⅓ full with vegetable oil. Heat until oil reaches 375°F. Deep fry coated jalapeños until golden (1½ minutes). Serve poppers with sour cream and salsa.

Kathleen K. Sanderson

Southwestern Strip Steaks

Serves 8

Eight 6-ounce strip or rib steaks

2 tablespoons chili powder (toasted)

1 tablespoon ground cumin

1 tablespoon onion powder

1½ teaspoons garlic powder

1 teaspoon ground red pepper

1 teaspoon dry oregano

Salt

Guacamole and salsa

Flour tortillas

Combine spices and blend well. Divide spice mixture among the steaks and rub into their surface. Let meat stand at least 2 hours or overnight, refrigerated.

Sprinkle meat with salt. Broil steaks 3 to 4 minutes on each side for medium rare, or pan fry in a very hot dry skillet for 3 to 4 minutes per side. Let meat rest 5 minutes before slicing and serving with guacamole, salsa, sour cream, and flour tortillas.

Kathleen K. Sanderson

The key to enjoying your own party is to make as much ahead as possible. Make the poppers a day before and fry them just as your guests arrive. Make the salsa and guacamole ahead, place in bowls, and cover with plastic wrap. Dry rub the meat ahead.

Guacamole

2 ripe Haas avocados

2 plum tomatoes, seeded and diced

2 scallions, diced

¼ cup cilantro, chopped

1½ to 2 tablespoons lemon juice

Dash of Tabasco sauce, to taste

Salt to taste

Slice avocados in half. Remove the pit and scoop out the flesh with a spoon. In a bowl using the back of a fork, mash avocados. Add tomatoes, scallions, cilantro, Tabasco, and lemon juice. Mix to combine and season to taste.

Kathleen K. Sanderson

Salsa Cruda

One 28-ounce can tomatoes, drained and chopped

or

2½ cups fresh tomatoes, chopped

4 scallions, diced

1 red pepper, diced

1 jalapeño, minced

2 cloves garlic, minced

⅓ cup cilantro, chopped

3 tablespoons red wine vinegar

2 tablespoons olive oil

Salt to taste

In a bowl, combine tomatoes, scallions, red pepper, jalapeño, garlic, cilantro, and vinegar; mix well. Add oil, if desired, and season to taste.

Kathleen K. Sanderson

Bitter Greens and Citrus Salad

Serves 8 to 10

Combine lettuces in a salad bowl. Top with jicama, oranges, onions, and olives. When ready to serve, toss with citrus vinaigrette (recipe follows).

1 small jicama, peeled and julienned

3 navel oranges, peeled and sliced

1 red onion, sliced and soaked in cold water

1 head chicory lettuce, washed and torn

2 bunches watercress, washed

1 bunch arugula, washed

½ cup Nicoise olives

½ to ⅔ cup citrus vinaigrette

Citrus Vinaigrette

Makes about 1½ cups

In a bowl add citrus juice, mustard, and zest. Stir to combine. Slowly whisk in oils to create a dressing. Add cilantro and season to taste.

Kathleen K. Sanderson

¼ cup lemon juice

¼ cup orange juice

2 teaspoons each lemon and orange zest

1 tablespoon Dijon mustard

½ cup salad oil

⅓ cup olive oil

2 to 3 tablespoons cilantro, chopped

Salt and ground red pepper

Mexican Wedding Cookies

2 cups all-purpose flour

1 cup confectioners' sugar

½ teaspoon salt

1 cup pecans, finely chopped

1 cup sweet butter, softened

2 teaspoons vanilla

Confectioners' sugar for rolling

Preheat oven to 350°F.

Sift together flour, sugar, and salt. Stir in nuts. In a mixer equipped with a paddle, cream the butter. Add flour mixture and vanilla to the bowl and mix until dough creates a ball.

Pinch off 1 tablespoon of dough for each cookie and form it into a ball. Place balls 1 to 2 inches apart on a parchment-lined or lightly greased cookie sheet. Flatten balls slightly with the back of a spoon.

Bake cookies until light brown, 16 to 18 minutes. Cool cookies on a rack. Dust them generously with sugar while warm.

Cookies can be kept in an airtight container for 2 to 3 weeks.

Kathleen K. Sanderson

Sangria

2 oranges

2 lemons

1 lime

½ cup sugar

1 cup water

7 cups red or white wine

1 cup brandy

2 peaches, peeled and sliced

1 liter club soda, if desired

Slice all citrus fruit, reserving ends. In a saucepan, combine sugar and water and bring to a boil. Add citrus ends, reduce heat and simmer 3 to 4 minutes. Remove from flame. Let syrup cool, then strain, discarding citrus ends.

Combine sliced fruit, sugar syrup, wine, brandy, and club soda, if desired. Chill sangria or serve over ice.

Kathleen K. Sanderson

Have fun with the Sangria—add any kind of fruit you like. You're making a "simple syrup" here and flavoring it with the ends of the citrus fruits. This can be done several days ahead. Finish it off on the day of the party. If you are using club soda, add it just before serving.

DEB BARRETT is a professional baker, private chef, and caterer.

KATHIE FINN graduated from Peter Kump's professional program with a Blue Ribbon diploma. Following an apprenticeship in corporate dining, she has worked as a private chef and caterer.

Special Occasion Dinner

Deb Barrett

Kathie Finn

Grilled Salmon with Lemon, Herb, and Pine-Nut Butter

Mashed Potatoes with Goat Cheese and Chives (ABOVE)

Radicchio, Endive, and Frisee Salad with Pecan Vinaigrette and Camembert Crisp (LEFT)

Strawberry Linzer Tart

Grilled Salmon with Lemon, Herb, and Pine-Nut Butter

Serves 6

2 sticks unsalted butter, room temperature

Zest of one large lemon (or two small ones)

½ bunch chives, minced (about ⅓ cup)

2 tablespoons parsley, minced

¼ cup toasted pine nuts

Six 6-ounce salmon filets, skin on

⅓ cup vegetable oil

2 tablespoons lemon juice

Kosher salt and freshly ground black pepper

Prepare the compound butter by combining the first four ingredients in the bowl of a food processor. Process to combine thoroughly.

Remove the butter from the workbowl and add the pine nuts, mixing to combine. Place half the butter on a sheet of plastic wrap and form it into a small "sausage." Using the plastic wrap to help you, roll the package tightly and twist the ends to secure. Repeat with the remaining butter. (May be frozen at this point.)

To grill the salmon, preheat a grill pan (or gas grill). Place the vegetable oil, lemon juice, salt, and pepper in a shallow dish or pie plate. Run the flesh side of the salmon through the oil/seasoning mixture and place directly on the preheated grill.

Grill the salmon for 5 to 7 minutes, or until you can lift it easily from the grill. If it sticks, do not move it. When you can lift the salmon, give it a quarter turn to achieve a "grill mark" pattern. Grill for 3 to 4 more minutes. Turn the salmon over (skin-side-down) and cook for another 5 to 10 minutes, depending on the degree of doneness you prefer.

To serve, cut one stick of the compound butter into 6 equal rounds. Place a piece of salmon on each of six serving plates and top it with a round of compound butter. The fish should be warm enough to begin to melt the butter.

Kathie Finn

Mashed Potatoes with Goat Cheese and Chives

Serves 6

Place the potatoes in cold water to cover. Over medium high heat, bring to a boil; reduce the heat and simmer the potatoes over medium to low heat. Cover the potatoes while cooking with the lid slightly ajar. Cook the potatoes until they are easily pierced with a knife.

Drain the potatoes. In the same "hot pot," add ¼ cup of the half & half and 3 ounces of the goat cheese. Return the drained potatoes to the pot and mash coarsely with a large serving fork or a potato masher. Add 1 teaspoon Kosher salt and the chives. Taste for seasoning. If you desire more goat cheese flavor, add the remaining 3 ounces of goat cheese. To achieve a smoother consistency, add the remaining ¼ cup of half & half. The potatoes may be prepared one day ahead up to this point.

To do ahead, store the potatoes in a lightly buttered casserole (preferably one with a lid). Cover the potatoes with buttered plastic wrap and refrigerate. Bring to room temperature before reheating in a 300°F. oven.

NOTE: The amount of goat cheese, half & half, and chives you use in this recipe depends on your individual taste! Feel free to experiment with the quantities given here until you find the combination that's right for you.

Kathie Finn

2 pounds Yukon Gold potatoes, peeled and cubed

3 to 6 ounces soft goat cheese, room temperature

¼ to ½ cup half & half cream

½ cup snipped chives (one good size bunch)

Kosher salt

Unsalted butter (optional)

Radicchio, Endive, and Frisee Salad with Pecan Vinaigrette and Camembert Crisp

Serves 6

PECAN VINAIGRETTE

2 tablespoons sherry vinegar

2 teaspoons sugar

Kosher salt to taste

6 tablespoons olive oil

½ cup pecans

CAMEMBERT CRISP

4 sheets phyllo

½ cup clarified butter

2 tablespoons honey mustard

2 small wheels camembert, rind removed, each round cut into 4 "triangles"

SALAD

1 large head radicchio, washed, well dried, and torn into bite-size pieces (tough white ribs removed)

1 large (or 2 small) Belgian endive, sliced ¼-inch thick

1 head frisee, washed, dried, and torn into bite-size pieces

Belgian endive turns green and bitter when exposed to light, so keep it wrapped in a paper towel and in a plastic bag in your refrigerator until you're ready to use it.

Begin making the vinaigrette by preheating the oven to 350°F.

Whisk together the sherry vinegar, sugar, and salt. Add the olive oil slowly, whisking to emulsify.

Place the pecans on a cookie sheet and toast for 10 to 15 minutes or until fragrant. Remove from the oven and add the hot pecans to the vinaigrette. Set aside.

Prepare the camembert crisp by stacking 4 sheets of phyllo dough on a cutting board so the long side is facing you. Lifting up ½ of the top sheet, brush the bottom sheet lightly with some of the clarified butter. Repeat with the other side.

Cut the phyllo into six equal lengthwise strips. Brush the bottom corner of each strip with some of the honey mustard. Place a piece of camembert on top of the honey mustard. Using a "flag fold," fold the phyllo to encase the camembert securely. Do not fold too tightly. Brush the finished triangle with melted butter. Repeat with the remaining phyllo and camembert for a total of 6 triangles. (May be prepared 4 to 5 hours ahead up to this point. Bring to room temperature before continuing.)

Preheat the oven to 400°F. On a parchment-lined baking sheet, bake the camembert crisps for 15 to 20 minutes until puffed and golden brown. Remove from the oven and let rest 5 minutes before serving.

Assemble the salad by combining the radicchio, endive, and frisee in a large salad bowl. Toss lightly with the dressing; place on salad plates, making sure each serving gets some pecans. Serve with the warm camembert crisp.

Deb Barrett

Strawberry Linzer Tart

**Makes 10-inch Tart
Serves 10 to 12**

For the filling, start with a zesting tool and remove the citrus zests. Set aside.

Remove the white pith from the orange and lemon. Seed the fruit and cut into small cubes. Clean and coarsely chop the strawberries. Place all of the fruit, along with the ginger, sugar, and ½ of the citrus peel, in a heavy-bottomed pot. Bring this mixture to a boil over moderate heat, stirring constantly. Cook until the fruit mixture is very thick, almost a preserve consistency. Add the vanilla and transfer to a bowl to cool. This can be made ahead and will keep in the refrigerator for 3 days.

To make the dough, preheat the oven to 325°F. Toast the nuts in a shallow pan for about 10 minutes. Transfer the nuts to a cool pan or platter and allow to cool completely.

Place the nuts and ½ cup flour in a food processor. Grind the mixture until the nuts are finely ground and the mixture starts to clump. Add the remaining flour, salt, and spices, and blend well. The mixture should look cakey.

Place the butter, sugar, and citrus zests in the large bowl of an electric mixer. Mix on medium speed until well blended. Add the yolks and vanilla and mix to incorporate. On low speed, add the flour and nut mixture ½ at a time, mixing until it forms a dough.

Remove ⅓ of the dough and shape it into a disk. Shape the remaining dough into a larger disk. Dust the disks with flour, cover with plastic wrap, and chill for 15 to 20 minutes.

Generously butter a 10-inch tart pan with a removable bottom. On a pastry board, and between sheets of plastic wrap or waxed paper, roll out the larger pastry disk to about 11 inches. Peel off the top piece of wrap and lift the pastry with the remaining wrap and place wrap-side-up in the center of the tart pan. Peel off the wrap and fit the dough down into the pan. Press the dough up the sides of the pan using your thumbs. If the dough is sticky, dip your thumbs into flour. Chill this for 15 minutes.

Lightly flour a sheet of waxed paper. Place the smaller pastry disk on the paper, sprinkle with flour, and top with a second sheet of waxed paper. Roll the disk into a 10-inch circle. Place the dough on a cookie sheet and chill for 15 minutes.

FILLING

1 orange

1 lemon

1 teaspoon vanilla

2 pounds strawberries

1¼ cups sugar

2 tablespoons candied ginger, chopped

¼ teaspoon fresh ground pepper

DOUGH

1 cup unblanched almonds

½ cup blanched hazelnuts

1½ cups unsifted all-purpose flour

¼ teaspoon salt

1 teaspoon ground cinnamon

1 teaspoon ground ginger

¾ cup unsalted butter, at room temperature

½ cup granulated sugar

½ of the lemon and orange zests

2 egg yolks

1 teaspoon vanilla

GARNISH

3 tablespoons blanched slivered almonds

Preheat the oven to 375°F. Position the oven rack in the lower third of the oven. Place a large jelly-roll pan in the oven to preheat.

Pour the fruit mixture into the pastry-lined tart pan, smoothing it to level the top. Do not overfill.

Remove the smaller disk from the refrigerator and peel off the top piece of waxed paper. With a pizza wheel or a pastry wheel, cut the dough into strips, approximately ½ inch wide. Cover the dough again with waxed paper and invert it. Peel off the top sheet of waxed paper. Lift up each strip of dough using an offset spatula and arrange in a criss-cross pattern over the filling. Use the longest pieces for the widest part of the pan.

Brush the top of the dough with cold water and sprinkle 3 tablespoons of blanched slivered almonds over the tart.

Place the tart on the jelly-roll pan in the oven and bake for approximately 50 to 60 minutes, or until golden brown and the filling is bubbling. Remove from the oven and cool on a rack. Loosen the outer ring as soon as the tart is cool enough to handle. Allow the tart to rest for at least 4 hours before cutting.

NOTE: This dough recipe is adapted from *Great Pies & Tarts* by Carole Walter, Clarkson Potter/Publishers.

Deb Barrett

JEAN YUEH, a native of Shanghai, is a culinary consultant who teaches and writes about Asian cuisines. One of her cookbooks won a Tastemaker Award in the Oriental category. She has traveled to Thailand and Southeast Asia to study with noted chefs and teachers.

A Taste of Vietnam

Jean Yueh

Vietnamese Fried Spring Rolls (ABOVE)

Vegetable Platter

Grilled Marinated Pork with Shallot and Garlic (LEFT)

Vietnamese Fried Rice

Coconut Custard

Vietnamese Fried Spring Rolls

40 small dried 6-inch rice papers (banh trang)

½ cup sugar

Vegetable platter

Nuoc Cham (dipping sauce)

Cooking oil for frying

FILLING

1 ounce cellophane noodles

4 dried Chinese mushrooms

1 tablespoon dried tree ears

½ pound lean ground pork

½ pound shrimp, shelled, deveined, and minced

1 small onion, peeled and minced

2 shallots, peeled and minced

2 cloves garlic, minced

½ teaspoon ground black pepper

½ teaspoon salt or to taste

1 egg

The Vietnamese cuisine is a delicate interpretation of the influences of Chinese, Indian, French, and Thai.

In separate bowls, soak and cover cellophane noodles, mushrooms, and tree ears with boiling water for 10 to 15 minutes or until soft. Drain. Remove the hard stems from the mushrooms and squeeze them to extract the liquid. Mince the mushrooms and tree ears and cut cellophane noodles into ½-inch sections. In a bowl, combine all the filling ingredients and mix very well.

In a large bowl, dissolve sugar with 4 cups warm water. Place a dry towel on the table. Immerse a sheet of rice paper in the warm water and quickly remove it. Lay it flat on the towel. When the paper becomes pliable in a few seconds, it is ready to be wrapped.

Place 1 generous teaspoon of filling at the lower third of the wrapper. Shape the filling into a cylinder. Lift the lower edge over the filling. Fold one side of the wrapper over and then the other side in an envelope style. Roll from bottom to top into a roll. Continue until all the filling is used.

To fry the rolls, heat 1 or 2 large frying pans filled with 1 inch of cooking oil over medium heat. When the oil is warm, carefully place rolls in the oil without touching each other and do not overcrowd the pan. Fry slowly over moderate heat turning occasionally for 10 to 15 minutes or until the rolls are golden and crisp. Remove from the pan and drain on paper towels. Keep warm in a low temperature oven while frying the remaining rolls. Serve with vegetable platter and Nuoc Cham dipping sauce (recipes follow).

Jean Yueh

Vegetable Platter

Serves 6 to 8

A vegetable platter is often a part of the Vietnamese meal. The vegetables and herbs are arranged on a platter, and the diners help themselves to whatever they desire for wrapping cooked foods, then dip in Nuoc Cham and eat out of hand.

1 head of Boston lettuce, separated into individual leaves (or any soft lettuce leaves)

1 bunch fresh mint

1 bunch fresh coriander

1 bunch fresh basil

1 cucumber, thinly sliced

Nuoc Cham
Dipping Sauce

Makes about ½ cup

Mix all the ingredients together in a bowl.

Jean Yueh

2 cloves garlic, finely minced

½ teaspoon crushed red pepper or to taste

4 teaspoons sugar

5 teaspoons fresh lime juice or to taste

¼ cup fish sauce or to taste

6 tablespoons water

1 tablespoon finely shredded carrot (optional)

Grilled Marinated Pork with Shallot and Garlic

Serves 4 to 5

Bamboo skewers, soaked in water for at least two hours or longer

1 pound pork loin, partially frozen

MARINADE

3 cloves garlic, peeled

3 large shallots, peeled

2 teaspoons sugar

1 tablespoon fish sauce

1 tablespoon dry sherry

$\frac{1}{4}$ teaspoon five spice powder

$\frac{1}{2}$ teaspoon freshly ground black pepper

1 tablespoon cooking oil

Process garlic and shallots in a food processor until very finely minced. Mix with the remaining ingredients for marinade.

Partially frozen pork is easier to slice. Slice the pork into $\frac{1}{4}$-inch thick slices. Then mix thoroughly with the marinade and let it stand for $\frac{1}{2}$ hour or longer.

Heat a grill or a broiler until very hot. In the meantime, thread the pork slices onto the bamboo skewers. Grill quickly, turning once until the pork is just cooked, about 3 minutes, depending on the intensity of the heat and the size of the meat. If desired, serve with Nuoc Cham dipping sauce.

Jean Yueh

Vietnamese Fried Rice

6 cups cooked rice, cold (cooked ahead)

½ pound shrimp, shelled and deveined, washed and dried, mixed with ¼ teaspoon salt and 1 teaspoon dry sherry

¼ cup sesame seeds

1 medium onion, minced

4 shallots, minced

4 cloves garlic, minced

4 scallions, chopped

Half a red bell pepper, finely chopped

¼ cup lemon grass, finely minced

4 tablespoons cooking oil

½ teaspoon crushed red pepper or to taste

2 teaspoons sugar

3 tablespoons fish sauce

Freshly ground pepper to taste

Fresh coriander leaves for garnish

Toast sesame seeds in a frying pan over medium heat until golden. Remove the seeds from the pan.

Remove tough outer leaves from lemon grass, slice very thinly, and mince finely.

Heat the wok or frying pan until hot, add 1 tablespoon oil. When oil is hot, add shrimp and stir-fry until cooked. Remove from the wok.

Heat 3 tablespoons of oil in the wok until hot. Add onion, shallots, and garlic, and cook over medium heat until they are almost translucent. Add crushed red pepper flakes, scallion, red bell pepper, and lemon grass and cook for about 30 seconds. Add rice, sugar, and fish sauce, tossing to mix and cook until the rice is thoroughly heated. Return cooked shrimp and add half of the toasted sesame seeds and ground black pepper. Mix thoroughly and serve hot. Sprinkle on top with the remaining sesame seeds and garnish with coriander leaves.

Jean Yueh

Coconut Custard

CUSTARD MIXTURE

3 large eggs

1½ cups coconut milk

6 tablespoons sugar

⅛ teaspoon salt

CRISPY COCONUT TOPPING (OPTIONAL)

2 tablespoons butter

2 tablespoons sugar

4 tablespoons desiccated coconut shreds

Preheat oven to 350°F. Beat all the custard ingredients together just until well mixed. Pour into 4 small individual Pyrex bowls or ramekins (if you want to unmold the custard, spray the container with cooking oil before filling). Place them in a baking pan and fill the pan with hot water about halfway up the side of the ramekins. Bake in the preheated oven for about 50 minutes or until a toothpick comes out clean when inserted into the custard. Serve warm or cold.

To make the topping, melt the butter in a small saucepan. Add sugar and coconut shreds and stir until well mixed. Spread the mixture in a small baking pan (lined with aluminum foil for easy cleaning) and bake 350°F. for about 10 minutes or until golden. Let it cool to room temperature. Sprinkle the topping on top of the custard and serve.

Jean Yueh

STEPHEN SCHMIDT is a cooking teacher, food historian, and a regular contributor to *Cook's Illustrated* magazine. He is the author of *Master Recipes* and is currently working on *Dessert in America*, a baking book and history of American dessert. Schmidt was also a major contributor to the new edition of *The Joy of Cooking*.

Easter Ham Dinner

Stephen Schmidt

Crab Cakes with Basil Puree (ABOVE)

Crusty Baked Ham with Apple-Fig Chutney

Gingered Spinach

Souffléed Lemon Tartlets with Raspberry Sauce (LEFT)

Crab Cakes with Basil Puree

CRAB CAKES

1 large egg white

2 tablespoons strained fresh
lemon juice

1½ teaspoons dry mustard

½ teaspoon Worcestershire
sauce

⅛ to ¼ teaspoon cayenne
pepper or to taste

¼ teaspoon salt

¼ teaspoon white pepper,
preferably freshly ground

½ cup good quality
commercial mayonnaise

3 tablespoons very finely
minced scallions, including
tender green parts

1 tablespoon very finely
minced fresh parsley

1 pound fresh cooked
crabmeat, preferably lump or
backfin, carefully picked over
to remove any shell or
cartilage

2⅓ cups fine dry bread crumbs

2 large eggs

½ teaspoon water

6 tablespoons (¾ stick) butter,
preferably unsalted

BASIL PUREE

1 cup very firmly packed fresh
basil leaves

2 tablespoons water

4 to 5 tablespoons extra-virgin
olive oil

½ teaspoon salt

Drops of fresh lemon juice

Combine egg white, lemon juice, dry mustard, Worcestershire sauce, cayenne pepper, salt, and white pepper in a mixing bowl and beat with a fork until blended. Stir in the mayonnaise, minced scallions, and parsley. Using a rubber spatula, gently fold in the crabmeat and 3 tablespoons of the bread crumbs, being careful to leave the crab in the largest possible pieces.

Sprinkle 1 cup of the remaining bread crumbs on a 16-inch sheet of waxed paper. To form each cake, drop a scant 3 tablespoons of the crab mixture onto the crumb-strewn waxed paper, flipping it once to coat both sides with crumbs and gently patting it into a disc about 1½ inches wide and ¾ inch thick. (The crab mixture will be quite soft. Don't worry if the cakes look messy at this point—they will have a final shaping later.) As each cake is formed, transfer it to a waxed paper-lined baking sheet with a spatula; you want to make 16 crab cakes altogether. Cover the cakes loosely with waxed paper and refrigerate for at least 30 minutes—an hour or more would be better—to firm.

Sprinkle another cup of bread crumbs on a fresh sheet of waxed paper. Beat the eggs and water in a bowl until foamy. One at a time, dip the cakes in the beaten egg, then dredge in a second coating of crumbs, pressing the crumbs in lightly and gently patting the cakes into shape. Add more crumbs to the waxed paper if needed. At this point, the cakes may be transferred to a plate, covered, and refrigerated for up a day before frying.

Melt enough butter in a heavy-bottomed 10- to 12-inch skillet to cover the bottom by ⅛ inch. Over a moderately high flame, heat the butter until it is fragrant and just beginning to color. Arrange one well-spaced layer of crab cakes in the skillet and sauté over moderate heat for 3 to 5 minutes per side, or until nicely browned. Turn the cakes carefully, as they are delicate. Keep the finished crab cakes warm in a very low temperature oven while you prepare the rest.

To make the basil puree, drop the basil leaves into 2 quarts of boiling water, wait 5 seconds, and then skim off the leaves and toss them into a bowl of ice water. Let stand until thoroughly cooled, then drain and blot well with paper towels. Combine the basil, 2 tablespoons of water, and 4 tablespoons olive oil in a blender and puree thoroughly, adding a bit more water and/or oil if the mixture is too thick to flow over the blades. Turn the puree into a small bowl and season with salt and a few drops of lemon juice. If you are not using the puree immediately, press a sheet of plastic wrap directly onto the surface and refrigerate.

To serve, cover the bottom of each plate with basil puree and arrange two (or four) crab cakes on top.

Stephen Schmidt

Crusty Baked Ham with Apple-Fig Chutney

Serves 8 to 10

One fully cooked smoked ham shank portion, weighing 6 to 7 pounds

1/3 cup port or Madeira

1/2 cup packed dark brown sugar

2 tablespoons dry mustard

1 tablespoon black pepper, freshly ground

1 teaspoon ground cloves

2 to 2 1/2 cups fresh, soft bread crumbs (8 to 10 ounces)

Dress up your Easter ham with this crunchy crust, and make the chutney up to a week ahead.

Preheat oven to 350°F.

Wash ham and pat dry. Cut away rind and flabby, discolored pieces of fat. Place ham cut-side-down on a rack in a roasting pan and bake at 350°F. until the thickest part registers 110°F. on a meat thermometer, about 1 1/2 hours.

Remove ham from roasting pan; spoon fat from pan and reserve. Pour wine into pan and scrape with a wooden spoon to dissolve browned bits; if necessary, set pan on a burner briefly. Mix brown sugar, mustard, pepper, and cloves, then stir in deglazing juices, making a thick paste; if too thick, add a little wine or water. Set ham cut-side-down on rack and return to pan. Score ham, except for flat side, through the fat and about 1/8 inch into the meat. Spread sugar paste on scored surfaces, then encrust thickly with bread crumbs, pressing them in with your hand. Drizzle crust with 2 to 3 tablespoons of reserved fat.

Increase oven temperature to 400°F. Bake ham for about 45 minutes, or until the crust is firm and nicely browned. Let ham rest 15 to 45 minutes, then carve perpendicular to the bone so that each slice will be covered with crust.

NOTE: Ham can be held 2 hours in a 150°F. oven.

Apple-Fig Chutney

5 ounces dried Calimyrna figs

1 teaspoon vegetable oil

1 pound Granny Smith apples, peeled, cut in 1/2-inch chunks

1/2 cup walnuts, very coarsely chopped

1/4 cup port or Madeira

Grated zest and strained juice of 1 lime

2 tablespoons sugar

1/4 teaspoon each salt and freshly ground black pepper

Remove stems from figs and cut in strips 1/4 inch wide, making about 1 cup. Add figs into a saucepan, cover with 1 cup water, and simmer until all water is absorbed. Set aside.

Over high flame, heat oil in a 9-inch nonstick skillet until it smokes. Add apples and walnuts and sauté, stirring frequently, until apples are barely tender. Both apples and walnuts should be dark, even a bit blackened. Add wine and boil off completely, then stir in figs, lime zest and juice, add sugar and cook briefly to glaze. Season with salt and pepper. Serve warm or at room temperature.

NOTE: Chutney may be refrigerated for 1 week.

Stephen Schmidt

Gingered Spinach

Serves 8

6 pounds fresh spinach

1- to 2-inch piece fresh ginger, depending on thickness

6 tablespoons unsalted butter

1½ teaspoons sugar, or more if needed

1 teaspoon salt, or more if needed

1 tablespoon strained fresh lemon juice, or more if needed

Remove all tough stems from the spinach and wash in several changes of water. Turn the spinach into a nonaluminum stockpot and set over moderately high flame. Stir until the spinach wilts into a mass, settling to the bottom of the pot. Lower the heat and continue to cook the spinach, uncovered, for 3 to 4 minutes, or until just tender but still bright green.

Turn the spinach into a colander and rinse under cold water until completely cooled. Press the spinach firmly with your hands to extract as much moisture as possible without crushing the leaves. Set spinach aside, or cover and refrigerate up to 2 days.

Peel the ginger, then cut crosswise, against the fibers, into paper-thin slices. Chop the ginger slices to a paste, or pound in a mortar, or puree in a mini-processor. Measure out 2 tablespoons of the pureed ginger, saving any extra for some other purpose. Heat the butter in a wide skillet or pot over moderate flame until melted and foamy. Add the ginger and cook, stirring, for 2 minutes. Add the spinach, toss to coat with butter, and cook slowly just until heated through. Season to taste with sugar, salt, and lemon juice, then serve at once.

Stephen Schmidt

Souffléed Lemon Tartlets with Raspberry Sauce

Serves 6

These gorgeous, delicious tartlets are really little lemon soufflés in pastry crusts, with tiny strings of homemade candied lemon zest on top. For an especially dramatic effect, present each one on a large white dinnerplate and drizzle the plate with shocking-red rivulets of raspberry sauce.

CANDIED LEMON ZEST

2 large to medium lemons

2 tablespoons confectioners' sugar

Begin by making the candied lemon zest. Wash the two lemons in hot water and dry well. Using a swivel-blade vegetable peeler, remove the zest (the colored part) of the lemons in long strips. Cut the zest lengthwise in the thinnest possible shreds—1/16 inch if you can manage it, but certainly no more than 1/8 inch. Cover the zest with at least 1 quart of water and simmer slowly, partially covered with a lid, for 20 to 25 minutes, or until it is very tender. Drain the zest in a sieve, flush with hot tap water, and firmly pat dry with paper towels. Turn into a bowl and toss with the confectioners' sugar. Zest will become moist and sticky, but it will dry out again as it stands. Set aside.

Set a rack in the center of the oven and preheat the oven to 375°F. Remove the tartlet shells from the molds and arrange on a baking sheet.

For the filling, separate the 3 whole eggs, turning the yolks into a heat-proof mixing bowl and the whites (without a speck of yolk mixed in) into a bowl suitable for your electric mixer. Set the whites aside. Add the 2 additional egg yolks to the three already in the bowl, sprinkle on ½ cup of the sugar, and whisk mixture until slightly thickened. Whisk in the lemon zest and juice. Fill a skillet roughly halfway with water and bring the water almost to a simmer; adjust the flame to maintain the water at this temperature. Set the bottom of the bowl containing the yolk mixture in the water bath and, stirring constantly, cook the mixture until thick enough to coat the spoon. This will take only a couple of minutes. Remove yolk mixture from the water bath and set aside.

With the mixer set at slow speed, beat the reserved whites until loose and foamy, then add the cream of tartar. Raise the mixer to medium speed, and beat the whites until they hold soft peaks. Raise the mixer to high speed, sprinkle on the remaining ¼ cup sugar, and beat the whites until stiff and glossy. Scoop the egg whites over the yolk/lemon mixture and fold in gently, but thoroughly, with a large rubber spatula.

Turn the filling into the shells, mounding it in the center, and bake the tartlets for 8 to 10 minutes, or until the filling has begun to brown and feels softly set in the center when gently patted. Do not overbake, or the tartlets will look shrunken and wrinkly when cooled. Let tartlets cool to room temperature on the baking sheet; the filling will deflate to its original volume.

Just before serving, strew the zest strips over the tops of the tartlets, then sprinkle lightly with confectioners' sugar, if you wish. Serve each tartlet with a little raspberry sauce spooned to the side.

For the sauce, whirl the berries in a blender or food processor until liquefied, then force the puree through a fine sieve to remove the seeds. Add enough sugar to make the sauce fairly sweet; the sweetness is needed to balance the tartness of the lemon filling.

NOTE: The candied zest may be made 3 days ahead. Seal in a plastic bag and store at room temperature. The tartlets may be made 1 day ahead; cover and set aside at room temperature. The raspberry sauce may also be prepared a day ahead; cover and refrigerate.

Stephen Schmidt

TARTLETS

6 baked tartlet shells made with Royal Pastry (recipe follows)

3 large eggs

2 large egg yolks

¾ cup sugar

1 tablespoon grated zest and ½ cup strained juice from the 2 lemons used above plus 1 additional lemon

⅛ teaspoon cream of tartar

RASPBERRY SAUCE AND GARNISH

1 cup fresh raspberries

¼ cup sugar

1 tablespoon strained fresh lemon juice

Confectioners' sugar in a shaker or sieve

Royal Pastry

Makes six 4½ × ¾-inch tartlet shells or one 9-inch pie shell or one 10 × 1-inch tart shell

Royal pastry is a special type of flaky pastry made with sugar and egg. In addition to imparting sweetness and a delightful crunch, the sugar and egg help the pastry to hold its shape during baking so that the crust does not buckle or slip down the sides of the pan. Royal pastry is a particularly good choice for tartlet crusts, which, because they are small, can ill afford to lose capacity due to shrinkage. It can also be used to make 10-inch tart crusts as well as crusts for tarte tatin and dessert pizzas.

1⅓ cups all-purpose flour

⅓ cup confectioners' sugar

½ teaspoon salt

8 tablespoons (1 stick) unsalted butter, cold

1 large egg, cold

2 teaspoons iced water

Combine the flour, sugar, and salt in a mixing bowl and blend thoroughly. Cut the butter into thin pats, then divide the pats in half. Add the butter to the dry ingredients and toss with your fingertips to coat. Firmly crush the butter into the dry ingredients with a pastry blender, periodically cleaning off the blender blades with a knife or rubber spatula. Stop blending as soon as the mixture looks something like oatmeal, with pea-size lumps scattered throughout.

If using a food processor, fit the machine with the steel blade. Combine the flour, confectioners' sugar, and salt in the workbowl and process briefly to blend. Cut the butter into pats, scatter over the dry ingredients, and give the mixture 8 to 12 1-second pulses, or until it looks like lumpy oatmeal. Turn mixture into a medium-size mixing bowl.

Beat the egg and iced water thoroughly with a fork in a small cup or bowl, then drizzle evenly over flour/butter mixture. Stir dough with the fork until little balls form, then press balls together with the back of the fork. Gather dough into a ball with your hands. Transfer dough to a sheet of plastic wrap, fold one side of the wrap over the dough, and flatten the dough into an inch-thick disc. Bring up the sides of the wrap to create an airtight seal. Chill dough for at least 1 hour before using.

Royal pastry sometimes breaks or cracks during rolling and forming. Should this occur, simply patch the offending spots with trimmings.

NOTE: The dough may be refrigerated for 2 days or, if sealed in an airtight plastic bag, frozen for 6 months.

Stephen Schmidt

Tartlet Shells

To form tartlet shells, have ready 6 tartlet molds about 4 inches wide and ½ inch deep, with a capacity of around ¾ cup.

Roll the pastry a little thicker than ⅛ inch, as for ordinary pie crust, then cut out 4 to 5 circles that are 6 inches in diameter, or wide enough to cover your molds. Ball up the scraps, reroll, and cut out 1 to 2 additional circles. Press the dough into the molds, then fold the protruding edges of the dough down to make the walls of the shells a double thickness. Firmly press the walls to fuse the two layers of dough.

Chill the shells for 30 minutes. Prick shells thoroughly with a fork and line with squares of aluminum foil, pressing the foil firmly against the bottom and sides. Prick foil with the fork in 6 places. Arrange shells on a baking sheet and return to the refrigerator for at least 30 minutes or for up to 24 hours.

Set a rack in the center of the oven and preheat the oven to 375°F.

Bake shells for 15 minutes with the foil liners in place, pressing down on the foil after 10 minutes, your hand protected by a paper towels, to flatten puffs. Carefully remove the liners and bake the shells for 10 to 12 minutes longer, or until they are nicely browned. Use shells as directed in your recipe.

Stephen Schmidt

MICHAEL PETERS is a graduate of the Paris Cordon Bleu. He is the former chef-proprietor of the premier-rated Brass Rail and has worked with French Michelin stars Michel Chabran, Marc Meneau, and Patrick Cirotte. He and his wife Marybeth Peters pioneered French bistro-style cooking in Morristown, NJ, opening the famous Pierre's, now located at 995 Mount Kemble Ave.

CAROLE WALTER, Certified Culinary Professional, is author of *Great Cakes*, a James Beard Award-winning cookbook. A consultant and teacher, she has appeared on many major network television shows. Carole studied patisserie and culinary arts in Austria, Denmark, France, and Italy.

Spring in Burgundy

Michael Peters

Carole Walter

Gougeres (LEFT)

Asperges Vinaigrette

Coq au Vin à la Bourguignonne

Peaches 'n Cherries in Port (ABOVE)

Gougeres
Cheese Puffs

½ cup milk

½ cup water

½ teaspoon salt

1 stick unsalted butter

1 cup sifted flour

4 eggs

2 ounces grated Gruyère cheese

Cayenne pepper

Put the milk, water, salt, and butter in a saucepan and bring to a boil. Remove from the heat and add the flour all at once. Stir with a wooden spoon until the flour has absorbed all the liquid.

Put back on the heat for a minute, stirring constantly. Add the eggs one at a time, making sure that they are well mixed to form a smooth paste. Add half the grated cheese and a little cayenne pepper.

Fill a ½-inch plain tipped piping bag with the "pate à choux." Pipe out little balls onto baking parchment. Sprinkle each with a little cheese.

Bake them at 400°F. for 10 minutes. Turn the heat down to 350°F. and finish baking them until they are golden brown, about another 15 minutes.

Serve them warm with aperitifs, preferably a glass of white burgundy.

Michael Peters

Asperges Vinaigrette
Asparagus Vinaigrette

Serves 4

1 pound fresh asparagus

3 tablespoons olive oil

1 teaspoon red wine vinegar

Juice of ½ lemon

Salt and pepper

1 hard-boiled egg, grated

½ red bell pepper, julienned

1 tablespoon fresh parsley, chopped

Butcher's twine

Trim and peel the coarse ends of the asparagus. Tie the asparagus in portion-size bundles with butcher's twine. Cook them in boiling salted water until just tender. Cool them in ice water. Let them drain on a towel. Untie and arrange them on plates.

Whisk together the olive oil, vinegar, lemon juice, salt, and pepper. Spoon a little over each portion of asparagus. Decorate each with the hard-boiled egg, julienned red pepper, and chopped parsley.

Michael Peters

Tying the asparagus in bundles makes it easy to blanch. Be sure to tie it in two places so it stays together. Peel the asparagus first if the stems are woody.

Coq au Vin à la Bourguignonne
Free Range Chicken in Red Wine

Serves 4

Cover the lardons with cold water and bring to a boil. Let simmer for 5 minutes; drain. Melt butter in large skillet; cook the lardons and pearl onions gently until they are a nice golden brown. Remove the lardons and onions, and cook the button mushrooms in the same butter. When they are lightly browned, remove them but keep the remaining butter.

Season the chicken with salt and freshly ground pepper. Brown the chicken pieces in the same butter that was used for the lardons, onions, and mushrooms. Sprinkle the chicken with the flour, stir, and place uncovered in a hot oven for 5 minutes to cook the flour. Remove the chicken from the oven, add the crushed garlic, and stir gently for 1 minute.

Add the wine, bouquet garni, onions, lardons, and mushrooms. Add enough of the chicken stock to barely cover the chicken. Cover and cook gently 45 minutes on top of the stove. Remove the pieces of chicken, vegetables, and the garni to a deep casserole. Reduce the sauce if it is too thin. Season with salt and pepper and strain the sauce over the chicken. If you like to be more authentic, you may sauté the liver in butter. Puree it in the food processor with the cognac and add it to the sauce at the end. This will add a lot of character.

Serve over hot, buttered noodles.

Michael Peters

One 3-pound free range chicken, cut in 8 pieces (keep the liver)

¼ pound button mushrooms

¼ pound slab bacon, cut into thick lardons

12 pearl onions

2 tablespoons flour

½ bottle red wine

2 cups chicken stock

2 cloves garlic, crushed

Bouquet garni: celery stalk, parsley, thyme, and bay leaf placed in a cheesecloth and tied

3 tablespoons cognac

2 tablespoons butter

1 pound wide egg noodles, cooked and buttered

Peaches 'n Cherries in Port

½ cup water

½ cup sugar

8 ripe peaches

1 pound washed and pitted
Bing cherries

2 slices lemon

1 cinnamon stick

¼ cup port wine

Make the sugar syrup by combining water and sugar in a small pot. Bring to a boil and simmer for 5 minutes. Set aside.

Peel and cut the peaches in half; discard the pits. To remove the skin, place peaches in a large bowl and pour boiling water over the top. Let stand about 1 minute, then drain off the hot water. Use the tip of a sharp paring knife to remove the skin.

Combine the sugar syrup, lemon, and cinnamon stick, in a large skillet. Bring to a slow boil. Add the peaches in a single layer, rounded side down. Cover and bring to a boil again, allowing the mixture to simmer 5 minutes. Turn the peaches. Add the cherries and port wine. Simmer 4 to 5 minutes longer. Remove the lemon. Cool and serve.

Carole Walter

KATHIE FINN graduated from Peter Kump's professional program with a Blue Ribbon diploma. Following an apprenticeship in corporate dining, she has worked as a private chef and caterer.

NICHOLAS MALGIERI, a Culinary Institute of America graduate, is the former executive pastry chef of Windows on the World. A nationally known teacher, his classes are sell-outs throughout the country. His two recent dessert cookbooks have garnered rave reviews.

Make Ahead Spring Entertaining

Junior Women's League of Morristown

Kathie Finn

Nicholas Malgieri

Roasted Tomato and Asparagus Salad with Goat Cheese and Balsamic Reduction

Lobster in Phyllo (ABOVE)

Grilled Chicken with Thai Green Curry Sauce

Pineapple Salsa

Wasabi "Smashed" Potatoes

Caramel Pecan Squares (LEFT)

Roasted Tomato and Asparagus Salad with Goat Cheese and Balsamic Reduction

Serves 6 to 8

This incredible combination of flavors is the perfect "do ahead" beginning for any meal. It can easily be turned into a main course by adding grilled chicken, lamb, salmon, or shrimp. When the weather warms up, grill the tomatoes and asparagus instead of roasting them.

VEGETABLES

12 plum tomatoes, halved, loose seeds removed

3 tablespoons olive oil, divided

1 teaspoon rosemary, minced

1 teaspoon thyme, minced

Kosher salt and freshly ground black pepper

1 ¼ pounds fresh asparagus, about ½ inch thick, bottom third removed

2 cups balsamic vinegar

LEMON VINAIGRETTE

¼ cup fresh lemon juice

½ teaspoon grated lemon zest

½ teaspoon Dijon mustard

½ to ¾ cup olive oil, vegetable oil, or grapeseed oil

Kosher salt and black pepper

TO SERVE THE SALAD

8 to 12 ounces mesclun

½ cup diced jicama

9 ounces crumbled mild goat cheese, room temperature

To roast the vegetables, preheat the oven to 350°F. Have ready 2 jelly-roll pans lined with baking parchment.

Place the tomatoes on one of the prepared pans, cut-side-up. Drizzle with 1½ tablespoons of the olive oil, then sprinkle with the minced herbs, Kosher salt, and fresh pepper. Roast for 35 to 40 minutes.

In a pie plate or other flat dish, combine the remaining olive oil with about 1 tablespoon of Kosher salt and a generous grind of black pepper. Toss the asparagus in the oil, turning to coat all of the spears well, and spread them out on the prepared pan. Roast the asparagus spears for about 25 minutes, or until they are easily pierced with the tip of a sharp knife. The roasting time will depend upon the thickness of the asparagus, so watch carefully.

While the vegetables are roasting, reduce the balsamic vinegar. Place the vinegar in a heavy-bottomed saucepan and bring to a boil. Reduce the heat and allow to simmer until reduced by about ⅔. The vinegar is done when you can tilt the saucepan and see a coating of the vinegar on the bottom. As it reduces, it will thicken and its flavor will intensify. Watch carefully! Let cool, store in a glass jar with a tight-fitting lid, and refrigerate. Bring to room temperature before using.

Make the lemon vinaigrette by whisking together the lemon juice, zest, and Dijon mustard. Add some Kosher salt and whisk to blend. Slowly drizzle in the oil, whisking constantly to form an emulsion. Taste for seasoning. Refrigerate in a glass jar with a tight-fitting lid.

To serve the salad, place the mesclun in a large bowl and toss with about ⅓ cup of the lemon vinaigrette. Arrange equal amounts of the mesclun on the "back half" of each salad plate.

Nestle 2 to 3 roasted tomato halves against the lettuce, then add several asparagus stalks. Sprinkle some diced jicama over the salad, then add the goat cheese. Drizzle the goat cheese and the vegetables with some of the reduced balsamic vinegar. Enjoy immediately, offering more of the lemon vinaigrette and reduced balsamic on the side.

NOTE: The vegetables may be roasted 1 day ahead. The balsamic vinegar and lemon vinaigrette may be made up to 3 days ahead. The jicama may be diced 1 day ahead. (Toss with a bit of the vinaigrette.) The goat cheese may be crumbled, covered tightly with plastic wrap, and refrigerated for several hours before serving.

Kathie Finn

Lobster in Phyllo

**Makes About 4 Dozen
Hors d'Oeuvres**

Make several dozen of these hors d'oeuvres and freeze them! They are a luxurious beginning to any evening, and make any occasion special. Serve with champagne, of course.

Melt 2 tablespoons of the butter in a medium skillet. Add the scallions and sauté over medium low heat for 2 to 3 minutes or until translucent. Add the lobster meat and the vermouth. Increase the heat to high, and stir to combine. Drain the mixture, reserving the liquid.

Add the remaining butter to the skillet and melt over low heat. Whisk in the flour and stir to combine. Cook for about 5 minutes, taking care not to let the flour brown. Add the reserved liquid, then whisk in the heavy cream. Stir constantly until the mixture begins to thicken. Add the reserved lobster meat, season to taste with salt and pepper, and set aside to cool. (May be made 1 day ahead.)

Assemble the triangles by having ready a jelly-roll pan lined with baking parchment. Place 2 sheets of phyllo on a cutting board or other flat surface. Lift the top sheet and brush the bottom sheet lightly with butter. Replace the top sheet and brush the edges with butter. Using a thin-bladed sharp knife or pizza cutter, cut the phyllo into 8 equal strips.

Place a small amount of the filling on the bottom of each strip, then fold each strip into a triangle using the "flag fold." Brush the top edge with a bit more of the butter before sealing the triangle. Place the completed triangles on the prepared jelly-roll pan and brush the tops lightly with butter.

1 steamed lobster (about 2 pounds), meat removed and finely chopped

4 tablespoons (1/2 stick) unsalted butter, divided

6 scallions, finely chopped (white and part of the green)

1/4 cup dry vermouth

1 1/2 tablespoons flour

1/4 cup heavy cream

Salt and pepper

1 cup clarified butter

12 sheets phyllo, preferably fresh

To freeze the hors d'oeuvres, place the phyllo on the jelly-roll pan in the freezer until frozen. Remove and wrap carefully in freezer paper or aluminum foil, placing wax paper between the triangles. You may also store the triangles in plastic containers with tightly sealed lids. Do not defrost before baking.

To bake the triangles, preheat the oven to 400°F. Line baking sheets or jelly-roll pans with baking parchment. Place the frozen phyllo about 2 inches apart on the prepared pans and bake for 12 to 15 minutes until puffed and golden. Let cool slightly before serving.

Kathie Finn, Adapted from Martha Stewart

Grilled Chicken with Thai Green Curry Sauce

The curry packs quite a wallop, so be discreet when using it. This sauce also works well with grilled shrimp, scallops, tuna, swordfish, and pork. It may be made up to 2 days ahead.

Make the sauce by melting the butter in a 10-inch sauté pan over medium heat. Add the ginger, lemon grass, and garlic and sauté for 2 minutes. Add the wine and, over high heat, reduce until only 2 tablespoons remain.

Add the coconut milk and curry paste, stirring to dissolve, and boil until reduced by half. Then add the fish fumet and reduce by ¾. Add the half & half, bring to a boil, then reduce the heat to medium and simmer for 10 minutes.

Place the sauce in a blender and mix on high speed, then strain and blend in the sugar. Season to taste with kosher salt. (May be made 2 days ahead up to this point. Let cool before covering the sauce with a piece of plastic wrap, then refrigerate. Bring to room temperature before gently rewarming over low heat.)

Grill the chicken by preheating a grill pan or gas grill.

Place the oil, salt, and pepper in a flat dish, such as a pie plate and stir to combine. Trim the chicken breasts of any visible fat or cartilage. Run each piece of chicken through the oil before placing it on the grill. (Do not crowd.)

Grill the chicken for about 3 to 4 minutes before giving it a quarter turn to achieve "hatchmarks." (If the chicken does not release easily, it is not ready to move.) Grill for another 3 minutes before turning and cooking on the other side. The chicken is done when it feels "springy" to the touch.

To serve this dish, you may place the chicken individually garnished with the herbs and a spoonful of the sauce, or you may place the grilled pieces on a platter, sprinkled with the julienned cilantro and mint and serve the sauce separately.

Kathie Finn

GREEN CURRY SAUCE

2 tablespoons unsalted butter

3 tablespoons peeled ginger, coarsely chopped

3 tablespoons lemon grass, coarsely chopped

1 clove garlic, coarsely chopped

1 cup dry white wine

2 cups coconut milk

2 tablespoons Thai green curry paste, or to taste

1 tablespoon fish stock, mixed with 1 cup warm water

1½ cups half and half

½ teaspoon light brown sugar

Kosher salt

CHICKEN

3 tablespoons flavorless salad oil

2 teaspoons Kosher salt

Freshly ground black pepper

8 skinless, boneless chicken breasts

GARNISH

Cilantro and mint leaves, well washed, dried, and julienned

Pineapple Salsa

This refreshing salsa is a welcome addition at any time of year. It is wonderful served with grilled fish, shrimp, chicken, or pork. For a change of pace, substitute 2 to 3 ripe mangoes for the pineapple. Or, mix and match!

1 ripe pineapple

⅓ cup diced red onion, or sliced scallions

⅓ cup diced red bell pepper

1 large jalapeño, seeded, deveined, and finely diced

½ cup cilantro leaves, chopped

¼ cup mint leaves, chopped

2 tablespoons lime juice

2 tablespoons vegetable oil

Kosher salt and black pepper

Using a sharp chef's knife, remove both ends from the pineapple. Remove the tough outer skin. Cut the pineapple into quarters and remove the core.

Cut half of the pineapple into ½-inch dice. (Reserve the remainder for another use.) Combine the remaining ingredients, seasoning to taste with salt and pepper. (Can be made 1 day ahead. Serve at room temperature.)

Kathie Finn

Wasabi "Smashed" Potatoes

Serves 6 to 8

Japanese wasabi is similar to our horseradish. Wasabi comes in tubes, and it is usually associated with sushi. Using it to flavor potatoes gives this ho-hum vegetable a welcome lift. It is quite spicy—so begin seasoning with small amounts!!

Wash and scrub the potatoes (do not peel). Halve or quarter any large potatoes. The pieces should be roughly the same size. Place in a large pot of cold water and bring to a gentle simmer over medium to high heat. Cook the potatoes until they are tender enough to be easily pierced with the tip of a sharp knife. Drain and return to the pot.

Combine the wasabi paste with the sour cream and add to the drained potatoes, then add the butter. Coarsely "smash" the potatoes with a large fork, blending in the wasabi, sour cream, and butter. The potatoes should still retain some of their shape and texture. Season to taste with Kosher salt and pepper. (May be done ahead up to this point.)

NOTE: To make moister potatoes, increase the sour cream and butter.

To make Sour Cream and Chive Smashed Potatoes, follow the recipe, eliminating the wasabi paste and adding ⅓ cup snipped chives. You may also add ¼ cup buttermilk or heavy cream.

TO MAKE AHEAD: Transfer the potatoes from the pot to a lightly buttered casserole. Place a sheet of buttered foil directly onto the cooled potatoes. (Refrigerate if not using within several hours. Bring to room temperature before continuing.) Rewarm the potatoes in a 300°F. oven and serve immediately.

Kathie Finn

2½ to 3 pounds new red potatoes

2 tablespoons wasabi paste, or more to taste

½ cup sour cream, room temperature

4 tablespoons (½ stick) butter, room temperature

Kosher salt and black pepper

Caramel Pecan Squares

This is a rich and easy recipe given to me by Jayne Sutton of Darien, Connecticut. I'm proud to say that Jayne has been coming to my classes for over 20 years, recently bringing her daughter Leslie, too.

COOKIE DOUGH

2 cups all-purpose flour

⅓ cup sugar

¼ teaspoon salt

1 teaspoon baking powder

8 tablespoons (1 stick) cold unsalted butter

2 large eggs

FILLING

12 tablespoons (1½ sticks) unsalted butter

¾ cup light brown sugar, firmly packed

3 tablespoons dark honey

Pinch salt

2 tablespoons heavy whipping cream

3 cups pecan halves or a mixture of halves and pieces

One 9 × 13 × 2-inch pan, buttered and lined with buttered parchment or foil

Set a rack in the middle level of the oven and preheat to 350°F. degrees.

For the dough, combine the flour, sugar, salt, and baking powder in the bowl of a food processor and pulse several times to mix. Cut the butter into about 16 pieces and add to the workbowl. Continue pulsing until the butter is finely worked into the dough and the mixture is a fine powder again. Add the eggs; continue pulsing until the dough forms a ball.

Place the dough on a floured surface. Roll into a roughly 9 × 13-inch rectangle. Fold the dough in half (to make it easier to handle) and transfer it to the prepared pan. Unfold the dough and press it out evenly over the bottom of the pan. Use the back of a spoon to smooth it if necessary. With your fingertips, press the dough about an inch up the sides of the pan all the way around. Chill the dough while you prepare the filling.

For the filling, combine the butter, brown sugar, honey, and salt in a medium saucepan and bring to a simmer, stirring occasionally with a metal spoon. Pour in the cream and allow the mixture to boil up once. Remove from heat and stir in the pecans. Let cool for about 15 minutes, then pour over the chilled crust. With the point of a spoon, spread the pecans evenly over the dough. Bake for about 25 to 30 minutes, or until the pastry is baked through and the filling is bubbling. Place on a rack until completely cooled.

Transfer the pastry to a cutting board and slide a long knife or spatula under it to loosen the paper or foil, then pull it away. Trim the edges, then use a ruler to mark, then cut, the pastry into 2-inch squares.

Nick Malgieri

Pecan pie in a cookie bar! Make sure you line the pan by placing the foil or parchment up the sides so you can easily grasp the foil to remove it from the pan. Give the foil a "hint" by first shaping it over the bottom of the pan. Butter it thoroughly.

BARBARA SEELIG-BROWN is a culinary educator, food writer, and nutritionist who's studied nutrition and exercise science at Fairleigh Dickinson University and The College of St. Elizabeth. She is a past board member of the American Heart Association in Somerset County and holds a certificate from the American Heart Association in nutrition. Currently the President of NYACP, a member of the IACP and the American Dietetic Association, Barbara completed her first cookbook, *Stress Free Cooking*.

Culinary Hearts: Spring Quickies

Barbara Seelig-Brown

Pasta with Truffle Oil

Fresh Baby Spinach with Shrimp

Snapper with Basil, Tomato, and Zucchini (ABOVE)

Chocolate Cream Cheese Roll with Fresh Berries and Cream (LEFT)

Pasta with Truffle Oil

1 small bottle truffle oil
(1 ounce)

1 large package mushrooms,
sliced

1 shallot, finely chopped

1 pound agnolotti pasta—
mushroom or pesto filled

Pepper mill

Extra-virgin olive oil (optional)

Cook pasta according to package directions.

Sauté mushrooms and shallot in some of the pasta cooking water or stock.
Mix with truffle oil to taste. Season with fresh ground pepper.

Extra-virgin olive oil may be added if desired.

Barbara Seelig-Brown

Fresh Baby Spinach
with Shrimp

Serves 4 to 6

1 pound large shrimp, shelled
and deveined

2 bags fresh baby spinach

1 clove garlic, minced

1 shallot, finely chopped

Chicken stock, homemade or
canned

½ cup fresh herbs such as
basil, oregano, parsley,
chopped

Good quality balsamic vinegar

Sauté garlic and shallot in small amount of chicken stock. Add fresh herbs
and spinach and mix well.

Add shrimp and cover. Cook a few minutes until shrimp turns pink. Add a
splash of good quality balsamic vinegar.

Barbara Seelig-Brown

Snapper with Basil, Tomato, and Zucchini

Serves 4

Marinate the fish in vinaigrette from 30 minutes to 2 hours.

Pour the olive oil into a heavy sauté pan. Heat on medium and sauté the shallot and zucchini.

When the zucchini is done to your liking, add the tomato and half the basil. Toss gently to just soften the tomato. Remove to a side plate.

Add the fish with enough marinade so that it doesn't stick to the pan. Sauté a couple of minutes on one side and then flip the fish over.

Add the zucchini mixture back into the pan and pour in the white wine. Cook until the fish flakes with a fork.

Barbara Seelig-Brown

1 pound-piece of snapper fillet or any other thick, white fillet

3 small zucchinis, sliced thin

1 large tomato

Large handful of fresh basil

1 shallot, chopped

1 tablespoon quality olive oil

1 cup white wine

1 bottle vinaigrette

Chocolate Cream Cheese Roll with Fresh Berries and Cream

⅓ cup all-purpose flour

⅓ cup powdered cocoa

¼ teaspoon baking soda

4 egg yolks

½ teaspoon vanilla extract

¾ cup granulated sugar, divided, ¼ cup and ½ cup

4 egg whites

8 ounces brick style Neufchâtel, (light cream cheese)

¼ cup honey

2 tablespoons almond liqueur

2 cups raspberries or strawberries

This light chocolate cake roll is filled with a delicious honey-almond light cream cheese. Served with fresh berries, it makes a perfect springtime dessert. Don't worry if the roll cracks—just dust it with a little extra powdered sugar.

This is a compilation of several recipes that add up to a great dessert, especially when made several hours ahead.

Preheat oven to 375°F.

Line a 15 × 10 × 1-inch baking sheet with parchment paper.

Stir together flour, cocoa, and baking soda. Set aside.

Beat egg yolks and vanilla in medium bowl on high speed of mixer for 5 minutes or until thick and lemon-colored. Gradually add ¼ cup of the granulated sugar, beating on high speed until sugar is almost dissolved.

Wash and dry beaters. Beat egg whites in large bowl on medium speed of mixer until soft peaks form (tips curl). Gradually add remaining ½ cup granulated sugar, beating until stiff peaks form (tips stand straight). Fold egg yolk mixture into beaten egg whites. Sprinkle flour mixture over egg mixture; fold in gently just until combined. Spread batter evenly in prepared pan.

Bake 12 to 15 minutes or until cake springs back when touched lightly. Immediately loosen edges of cake from pan; turn cake out onto a towel sprinkled with powdered sugar. Roll up towel and cake, jelly-roll style, starting from one of the cake's short sides.

Cool on wire rack.

To prepare filling, mix Neufchâtel with honey and almond liqueur in food processor until smooth. Carefully unroll cake and spread filling.

Slice berries, if large, and place over filling.

Roll cake and refrigerate until serving time. Garnish with fresh mint and additional berries, if desired.

Barbara Seelig-Brown

INGREDIENTS INDEX

RECIPE AUTHORS